inspiration 2

Elementary Companion

German Edition

Macmillan Education
Between Towns Road, Oxford, OX4 3PP, UK
A division of Macmillan Publishers Limited
Companies and representatives throughout the world

ISBN 13: 1 978 1 4050 8402 4
ISBN 10: 1 4050 8402 2

Text, design and illustration © Macmillan Publishers Limited 2006

First published 2006

All rights reserved; no part of this publication may be reproduced,
stored in a retrieval system, transmitted in any form, or by any means,
electronic, mechanical, photocopying, recording, or otherwise,
without the prior written permission of the publishers.

Designed by Anne Sherlock
Illustrated by Mark Davies

The publishers would like to thank Olivia Johnston for the Vocabulary *Extra!* exercises

Printed and bound by Martins the Printers Ltd

2010   2009
10 9   8   7   6   5   4   3   2

CONTENTS

WORDLIST

Unit 1	1
Unit 2	11
Unit 3	18
Unit 4	25
Unit 5	31
Unit 6	36
Unit 7	40
Unit 8	48
Grammar Summary	53
Alphabetical Index	62
Vocabulary *Extra!*	75

Welcome to the *inspiration* Companion 2

What information does the *inspiration* Companion 2 give you?
• a summary of key words and phrases from each unit of *inspiration* 2 Student's Book
• pronunciation of the key words and phrases
• translations of the key words and phrases
• sample sentences showing the words and phrases in context
• a translation of the Grammar Summary from *inspiration* 2 Student's Book
• alphabetical index
• listening activities to practice key words and phrases
• Macmillan English Dictionary 'Star rating'

Abbreviations used in the Companion

(art)	article	(phr v)	phrasal verb	(m)	masculine	(Am E)	American English
(v)	verb	(pron)	pronoun	(pl n)	plural noun	(TS)	Tapescript
(v*)	irregular verb	(prep)	preposition	(adv)	adverb		
(adj)	adjective	(det)	determiner	(conj)	conjunction		
(n)	noun	(f)	feminine				

VOWELS AND DIPHTHONGS

/ɪ/	big fish	/bɪg fɪʃ/	/ɑ:/	calm start	/kɑːm stɑːt/
/i:/	green beans	/gri:n bi:nz/	/ɒ/	hot spot	/hɒt spɒt/
/ʊ/	should look	/ʃʊd lʊk/	/ɪə/	ear	/ɪə/
/u:/	blue moon	/blu: mu:n/	/eɪ/	face	/feɪs/
/e/	ten eggs	/ten egz/	/ʊə/	pure	/pjʊə(r)/
/ə/	about mother	/əbaʊt mʌðə/	/ɔɪ/	boy	/bɔɪ /
/ɜ:/	learn words	/lɜ:n wɜ:dz/	/əʊ/	nose	/nəʊz/
/ɔ:/	short talk	/ʃɔ:t tɔ:k/	/eə/	hair	/heə/
/æ/	fat cat	/fæt kæt/	/aɪ/	eye	/aɪ/
/ʌ/	must come	/mʌst kʌm/	/aʊ/	mouth	/maʊθ/

CONSONANTS

/p/	pen	/pen/	/s/	snake	/sneɪk/
/b/	bad	/bæd/	/z/	noise	/nɔɪz/
/t/	tea	/ti:/	/ʃ/	shop	/ʃɒp/
/d/	dog	/dɒg/	/ʒ/	measure	/meʒə(r)/
/tʃ/	church	/tʃɜ:tʃ/	/m/	make	/meɪk/
/dʒ/	jazz	/dʒæz/	/n/	nine	/naɪn/
/k/	cost	/kɒst/	/ŋ/	sing	/sɪŋ/
/g/	girl	/gɜ:l/	/h/	house	/haʊs/
/f/	far	/fa:(r)/	/l/	leg	/leg/
/v/	voice	/vɔɪs/	/r/	red	/red/
/θ/	thin	/θɪn/	/w/	wet	/wet/
/ð/	then	/ ðen/	/j/	yes	/jes/

Unit 1

This is YTV (pp. 6–7)

American (adj)	/əˈmerɪkən/	amerikanisch; Amerikaner(in)	Ben is **American** – he's from New York.
answer (n)★★★	/ˈɑːnsə/	Antwort	Call us with your **answer** today!
Australia (n)	/ɒsˈtreɪliə/	Australien	Melbourne is a big city in **Australia**.
boy (n)★★★	/bɔɪ/	Junge	These are the winners – four girls and four **boys**.
Brazil (n)	/brəˈzɪl/	Brasilien	Pedro is from Rio de Janeiro in **Brazil**.
call (= telephone) (v)★★★	/kɔːl/	anrufen	**Call** us on 0800 444 796 if you live in the UK.
call (= name someone/something) (v)	/kɔːl/	nennen	Tomasz's friends **call** him Tomek for short.
competition (n)★★★	/kɒmpəˈtɪʃən/	Wettbewerb; Preisausschreiben	Eight people won the holiday **competition**.
English (adj)	/ˈɪŋglɪʃ/	englisch; Engländer(in)	Carol is from York and she's **English**.
friend (n)★★★	/frend/	Freund(in)	What do Tomasz's **friends** call him?
from (prep)★★★	/frɒm/	wo...her?; aus	"Where is Pedro **from**?" "He's **from** Brazil."
holiday (n)★★★	/ˈhɒlɪdeɪ/	Urlaub	The prize is a **holiday** in London.
Poland (n)	/ˈpəʊlənd/	Polen	Tomasz is from Warsaw in **Poland**.
population (n)★★★	/pɒpjʊˈleɪʃən/	Bevölkerung	What is the **population** of Greater London?
presenter (n)	/prɪˈzentə/	Moderator(in)	The YTV **presenter** is called Paula.
prize (n)★★	/praɪz/	Preis	The **prize** for the winners is a holiday in London.
river (n)★★★	/ˈrɪvə/	Fluss	London's **river** is called the Thames.
for short	/fə ˈʃɔːt/	kurz; einfach	My name is Tomasz but my friends call me Tomek **for short**.
Spain (n)	/speɪn/	Spanien	Hi! I'm Laura and I'm from **Spain**.
Spanish (adj)	/ˈspænɪʃ/	spanisch; Spanier(in)	Laura's **Spanish** – she's from Barcelona.
Swiss (adj)	/swɪs/	Schweizer(in)	Hi! My name's Gabi and I'm **Swiss**.
Switzerland (n)	/ˈswɪtsələnd/	die Schweiz	Gabi is from **Switzerland**.
week (n)★★★	/wiːk/	Woche	There are seven days in a **week**.
win (v)★★★	/wɪn/	gewinnen	**Win** a week in London!
winner (n)★★	/ˈwɪnə/	Gewinner	The photo shows the eight **winners** of the holiday competition.

1 Do you really speak Chinese? (pp. 8–9)

aerobics (n)	/eə'rəubɪks/	Aerobic	Carol does **aerobics** every Tuesday.
bed (n)★★★	/bed/	Bett	What time do you go to **bed**?
bird (n)★★★	/bɜ:d/	Vogel	The **birds** in Trafalgar Square are pigeons.
breakfast (n)★★	/'brekfəst/	Frühstück	English people often drink tea for **breakfast**.
chat (v)★★	/tʃæt/	chatten	Jack **chats** to people online.
cinema (n)★★	/'sɪnəmə/	Kino	Sally goes to the **cinema** every Saturday.
computer (n)★★★	/kəm'pju:tə/	Computer	Do you like playing on **computers**?
correct (adj)★★★	/kə'rekt/	korrekt	You get one point for a **correct** answer.
different (adj)★★★	/'dɪfrənt/	anders	I don't play on my computer. I chat to people online – that's **different**.
drink (v)★★★	/drɪŋk/	trinken	Do you **drink** a lot of tea?
eat (v)★★★	/i:t/	essen	Do you like **eating** fish and chips?
evening (n)★★★	/'i:vnɪŋ/	Abend	She goes swimming on Friday **evening**.
every (adj)★★★	/'evri/	jeder, -e, -es	Sally goes to the movies **every** Saturday.
film (n)★★★	/fɪlm/	(Spiel)film	I often go to the cinema to see **films**.
fish (n)★★★	/fɪʃ/	Fisch	**Fish** and chips is a popular British meal.
football (n)★★	/'futbɔ:l/	Fußball	I play **football** on Friday and Saturday.
good (adj)★★★	/gud/	gut	Do you know any **good** jokes?
How about ...?	/haʊ əbaʊt/	Wie ist es mit ...?	"What things do you like? **How about** computers?" "No, I don't like computers."
know (v)★★★	/nəu/	kennen	Do you **know** any good jokes?
joke (n)★	/dʒəuk/	Witz	Carol doesn't really speak Chinese – it's just a **joke**.
language (n)★★★	/'læŋgwɪdʒ/	Sprache	Carol speaks three **languages** – English, Italian and French.
late (adv)★★★	/leɪt/	spät	I often go to bed **late**.
like (v)★★★	/laɪk/	mögen	Carol doesn't **like** pigeons at all.
look (at) (v)★★★	/luk (ət)/	anschauen; ansehen	**Look** at those birds!
love (v)★★★	/lʌv/	lieben	Sally **loves** the pigeons in Trafalgar Square.
the movies	/ðə 'mu:vɪz/	Kino	"How often do you go to **the movies**?" "Once a week."
of course (not)★★★	/əv 'kɔ:s (nɒt)/	natürlich nicht	"Do you really speak Chinese?" "**Of course** not!"
online (adv)	/'ɒnlaɪn/	online	You can chat to people **online** on a computer.
phone (v)★★★	/fəun/	telefonieren mit	She often **phones** her friends.
pigeon (n)	/'pɪdʒɪn/	Taube	Carol, Sally and Jack are looking at the **pigeons**.
play (v)★★★	/pleɪ/	spielen	Carol never **plays** on computers.

point (n)★★★	/pɔɪnt/	Punkt	Correct answer! One **point**!
sea monster (n)	/ˈsiː ˌmɒnstə/	Meeresungeheuer; Seemonster	Jack tells a joke about **sea monsters**.
ship (n)★★★	/ʃɪp/	Schiff	A **ship** is a large boat that travels across the sea.
speak (v)★★★	/spiːk/	sprechen	How many languages do you **speak**?
spell (v)★	/spel/	schreiben; buchstabieren	How do you **spell** 'aerobics'?
swimming (n)	/ˈswɪmɪŋ/	Schwimmen	She goes **swimming** every Friday evening.
tea (n)★★★	/tiː/	Tee	**Tea** is a very popular drink in Britain.
teach (v)★★★	/tiːtʃ/	unterrichten	Carol's mum **teaches** aerobics.
thing (n)★★★	/θɪŋ/	Sache	What sort of **things** do you like?
watch (v)★★★	/wɒtʃ/	fernsehen	Ben **watches** TV every evening.

2 You're standing on my foot! (pp. 10–11)

badge (n)	/bædʒ/	Abzeichen; Button	Greg, the tour guide, is wearing a YTV **badge**.
bag (n)★★★	/bæg/	Tasche	The tall man is putting his hand inside the girl's **bag**.
behind (prep)★★★	/bɪˈhaɪnd/	hinter	Who's standing **behind** the girl in red?
busker (n)	/ˈbʌskə/	Straßenmusikant	You can see a photo of a **busker** playing a guitar in Covent Garden.
camera (n)★★★	/ˈkæmrə/	Kamera	Gabi is helping Pedro with his **camera**.
everyone (pron)★★★	/ˈevrɪwʌn/	alle	The tour guide tells **everyone** about Covent Garden.
fleece (n)	/fliːs/	Fleecejacke; Flausch	Ben is wearing an orange **fleece**.
flower (n)★★★	/ˈflaʊə/	Blume	Can you see the pink and white **flowers** in the photo?
girl (n)★★★	/gɜːl/	Mädchen	Four of the winners of the holiday competition are **girls**.
group (n)★★★	/gruːp/	Gruppe	The YTV **group** are sightseeing in Covent Garden.
guitar (n)★★★	/gɪˈtɑː/	Gitarre	The man playing the **guitar** is a busker.
happen (v)★★	/ˈhæpən/	geschehen	What's **happening**? I can't see a thing.
hat (n)★★	/hæt/	Hut	A tall man is standing behind the girl in the red **hat**.
help (v)★★★	/help/	helfen	Gabi's **helping** him with his camera.
hold hands	/həʊld ˈhændz/	Händchen halten	"Are Pedro and Gabi **holding hands**?" "No, they're not."
jacket (n)★★	/ˈdʒækɪt/	Jacke; Jackett	The busker is wearing a black **jacket**.
jeans (n pl)★★	/dʒiːnz/	Jeans	How many people in the photo are wearing **jeans**?
Let me see.	/let miː ˈsiː/	Lass mich sehen.	You're standing in front of me. **Let me see**.
listen (to) (v)★★★	/ˈlɪsən (tə)/	zuhören	Ben isn't **listening** to Greg. He's watching the tall man.
man (pl men) (n)	/mæn/ (/men/)	Mann	The tall **man** is putting his hand in the girl's bag.

map (n)★★★	/mæp/	Karte	Laura and Tomek are looking at a **map**.
mean (v)★★★	/miːn/	meinen	"What's that man doing?" "Who do you **mean**?"
next to★★★	/neks tə/	neben	Laura is standing **next to** the tour guide.
pullover (n)	/ˈpʊləʊvə/	Pullover	Jack is wearing a blue **pullover**.
purse (n)★	/pɜːs/	Geldbörse; Portemonnaie	I think he's taking her **purse**.
put (v)★★★	/pʊt/	stecken	He's **putting** his hand in her bag.
Quick! (interj)	/kwɪk/	Schnell!	**Quick!** Let's stop him.
run (v)★★★	/rʌn/	laufen	Stop him! He's **running** this way.
see (v)★★★	/siː/	sehen	I can't **see** a thing. What's happening?
shirt (n)★★★	/ʃɜːt/	Hemd	Tomek is wearing an orange and white **shirt**.
shoe (n)★★★	/ʃuː/	Schuh	Ben and Carol are wearing brown **shoes**.
sightseeing (n)	/ˈsaɪtsiːɪŋ/	Besichtigungen; Stadtrundfahrt	Do you like **sightseeing**?
stand (v)★★★	/stænd/	stehen	Ow! You're **standing** on my foot!
steal (v)★★	/stiːl/	stehlen	Stop him! He's **stealing** her purse.
stop (v)★★★	/stɒp/	aufhalten	Let's **stop** him!
sweatshirt (n)	/ˈswetʃɜːt/	Sweatshirt	Who is wearing the green **sweatshirt**?
take (v)★★★	/teɪk/	nehmen	The tall man is **taking** her purse.
take photographs	/teɪk ˈfəʊtəˌɡrɑːfs/	Fotos machen	You use a camera to **take photographs**.
talk (about) (v)★★★	/tɔːk (əˈbaʊt)/	reden, sprechen von	I'm **talking** about the tall man standing behind the girl in red.
tell (v)★★★	/tel/	erzählen	Greg is **telling** everyone about Covent Garden.
top (n)★★★	/tɒp/	Top	Laura is wearing an orange **top**.
tour guide (n)	/tʊə ɡaɪd/	Reiseleiter	"Who's Greg?" "He's the **tour guide**."
trainer (n)	/ˈtreɪnə/	Sportschuhe; Turnschuhe	How many people are wearing **trainers**?
trousers (n pl)★★	/ˈtraʊzəz/	Hose	Ben, Greg and Laura are wearing beige **trousers**.
T-shirt (n)	/ˈtiːʃɜːt/	T-Shirt	Gabi is wearing a pink **T-shirt**.
umbrella (n)	/ʌmˈbrelə/	Regenschirm	Jack is the only person with an **umbrella**.
visit (v)★★★	/ˈvɪzɪt/	besuchen	Tomek is **visiting** London for the first time.
watch (v)★★★	/wɒtʃ/	beobachten	Jack and Sally are **watching** the busker.
wear (v)★★★	/weə/	tragen	The busker is **wearing** a black jacket.

3 What's the producer's job? (pp. 12–13)

actor (n)★★★	/ˈæktə/	Schauspieler	An **actor** plays a part in a film.
bangle (n)	/ˈbæŋɡəl/	Armreif	Carol is wearing **bangles** on her left arm.

boss (n)★★	/bɒs/	Boss; Vorgesetzte(r)	Greg's **boss** is called Kate Dixon.
briefcase (n)	/ˈbriːfkeɪs/	Aktentasche	There are two cups of coffee on the **briefcase**.
cameraman (n)	/ˈkæmrəmæn/	Kameramann	The **cameraman** shoots the film.
car crash (n)	/ˈkɑː kræʃ/	Autounfall	Stuntmen and stuntwomen do things like **car crashes** and fights.
in charge of★★★	/ɪn ˈtʃɑːdʒ əv/	verantwortlich für	I'm **in charge of** the film and I make sure it's good.
coffee (n)★★★	/ˈkɒfi/	Kaffee	Greg is drinking Kate's **coffee**!
coffee break (n)	/ˈkɒfi breɪk/	Kaffeepause	I'll tell you what we're doing during the actors' **coffee break**.
come (v)★★★	/kʌm/	kommen	**Come** and meet my boss!
dangerous (adj)★★★	/ˈdeɪndʒərəs/	gefährlich	Stuntmen and stuntwomen do **dangerous** things like fights and car crashes.
director (n)★★★	/dɪˈrektə, daɪˈrektə/	Regisseur	The **director** tells the actors what to do.
Excuse me.★★	/ɪkˈskjuːz miː/	Verzeihung; Entschuldigung	**Excuse me**, what are 'pickpockets'?
expensive (adj)★★★	/ɪkˈspensɪv/	teuer	The producer makes sure that the film isn't too **expensive**.
fight (n)★★★	/faɪt/	Kampf	Stuntmen and stuntwomen do things like car crashes and **fights**.
glasses (n pl)★★★	/ˈglɑːsɪz/	Brille	Kate Dixon, the YTV producer, is wearing **glasses**.
great (adj)★★★	/greɪt/	großartig; toll	I hope you're having a **great** time here in London.
have a great time	/ˌhæv ə greɪt ˈtaɪm/	eine tolle Zeit haben	I hope you're all **having a great time** in London.
Hey! (interj)★	/heɪ/	He!	**Hey**, Greg, you're drinking my coffee!
hope (v)★★★	/həʊp/	hoffen	I **hope** you're having a great time in London.
job (n)★★★	/dʒɒb/	Job; Aufgabe	"What's the producer's **job**?" "The producer is in charge of the film."
left (adj)★★★	/left/	linker, -e, -es	Jack's holding an umbrella in his **left** hand.
lights (n pl)★★★	/laɪts/	Beleuchtung; Scheinwerfer	Kate is standing just in front of the **lights**.
magazine (n)★★	/mægəˈziːn/	Zeitschrift; Magazin	"Is it Jack's **magazine**?" "No, it's Carol's."
make a film	/ˌmeɪk ə ˈfɪlm/	einen Film machen, drehen	We're **making a film** about tourists in London.
make sure that	/ˌmeɪk ʃʊə ðət/	darauf achten dass	Her job is to **make sure that** the film is good.
meet (v)★★★	/miːt/	kennen lernen	Come and **meet** my boss, everyone!
notebook (n)	/ˈnəʊtbʊk/	Notizbuch	Greg is holding a **notebook** in his hand.
pickpocket (n)	/ˈpɪkpɒkɪt/	Taschendieb	**Pickpockets** steal things from people's bags and pockets.
play (a part/role) (v)★★★	/pleɪ (ə pɑːt rəʊl)/	spielen	Actors **play** the different parts.
pocket (n)★★	/ˈpɒkɪt/	Tasche	A pickpocket stole a purse from my **pocket**.
problem (n)★★★	/ˈprɒbləm/	Problem	Pickpockets are a **problem** for tourists.
producer (n)★	/prəˈdjuːsə/	Produzent	Kate is a **producer** for YTV.
You're right.	/ˈraɪt/	Du hast Recht.	**You're right**, it's your coffee – it's got sugar in it!

scarf (n)	/skɑːf/	Schal	Greg is the only person wearing a **scarf**.
scriptwriter (n)	/ˈskrɪptraɪtə/	Drehbuchautor	The **scriptwriter** writes the film.
shoot (a film) (v)★★★	/ʃuːt ə fɪlm/	einen Film drehen	The cameraman **shoots** the film.
skirt (n)★★	/skɜːt/	Rock	Kate is wearing a grey **skirt**.
stuntman/stuntwoman (n)	/ˈstʌntmæn/ /ˈstʌntwʊmən/	Stuntman, Stuntgirl	The **stuntmen** and **stuntwomen** do dangerous things in a film.
sugar (n)★★	/ˈʃʊgə/	Zucker	This is your coffee – it's got **sugar** in it!
sunglasses (n pl)	/ˈsʌnglɑːsɪz/	Sonnenbrille	The woman in the blue denim jacket is wearing **sunglasses**.
tourist (n)★★	/ˈtʊərɪst/	Tourist	We're making a film about **tourists** in London.
watch (n)★★	/wɒtʃ/	Armbanduhr	Tomek is wearing a **watch** on his right hand.
write (v)★★★	/raɪt/	schreiben	"Who **writes** the film?" "The scriptwriter."

4 Integrated skills: Personal profiles (pp. 14–15)

again (adv)★★★	/əˈgen/	wieder	He's looking forward to seeing his girlfriend **again**.
angry (adj)★★★	/ˈæŋgri/	böse; zornig	People who don't listen make me **angry**.
baseball cap (n)	/ˈbeɪsbɔːl kæp/	Baseballmütze; -käppchen	Ben is wearing a blue **baseball cap**.
before (prep)★★★	/bɪˈfɔː/	vor	He cycles five kilometres **before** breakfast.
book (n)★★★	/bʊk/	Buch	I'm reading an English **book** called *L.A. winners*.
boyfriend (n)★	/ˈbɔɪfrend/	Freund	Does Gabi have a **boyfriend**?
clothes (n pl)★★★	/kləʊðz/	Kleidung	His favourite **clothes** are shorts and his baseball cap.
colour (n)★★★	/ˈkʌlə/	Farbe	Her favourite **colour** is pink.
cycle (v)	/ˈsaɪkəl/	Rad fahren	Tomek **cycles** five kilometres before breakfast.
It depends.★★★	/ɪt dɪˈpendz/	Es kommt darauf an.	"What are your favourite clothes?" "**It depends**."
dictionary (n)	/ˈdɪkʃnri/	Wörterbuch	If you don't understand a word, use a **dictionary**.
difficult (adj)★★★	/ˈdɪfɪkəlt/	schwierig	That's a **difficult** question.
dog (n)★★★	/dɒg/	Hund	Ben relaxes by playing with his **dog**.
easy (adj)★★★	/ˈiːzi/	leicht; einfach	"What's your favourite colour?" "That's **easy**. Pink."
favourite (adj)★★	/ˈfeɪvrət/	Lieblings-	What are Ben's **favourite** clothes?
finally (adv)★★★	/ˈfaɪnəli/	schließlich; zum Schluss	**Finally**, Ben watches TV for half an hour every evening.
find out (phr v)	/faɪnd ˈaʊt/	herausfinden	**Find out** what Gabi is like by reading about her.
girlfriend (n)★	/ˈgɜːlfrend/	Freundin	Tomek has a **girlfriend**.
guess (v)★★	/ges/	raten	Can you **guess** what the word means?

half an hour	/hɑːf ən 'aʊə/	eine halbe Stunde	He watches TV for **half an hour** every evening.
happy (adj)★★★	/'hæpi/	glücklich	Sunshine and blue sky make me **happy**.
at home	/ət 'həʊm/	zu Hause	Ben lives **at home** with his parents and sister.
important (adj)★★★	/ɪm'pɔːtənt/	wichtig	Is there someone who is very **important** to you?
learn (v)★★★	/lɜːn/	lernen	I'm **learning** English at the moment.
live (v)★★★	/lɪv/	wohnen; leben	"Where do you **live**?" "In Zurich, in Switzerland."
look forward to (phr v)	/lʊk 'fɔːwəd tə/	sich freuen auf	Tomek is **looking forward to** seeing his girlfriend again.
miss (v)★★★	/mɪs/	vermissen	I **miss** my friends now I'm in London.
mistake (n)★★	/mɪs'teɪk/	Fehler	There are six **mistakes** in Ben's profile.
nothing (pron)★★★	/'nʌθɪŋ/	nichts	"What makes Ben angry?" "**Nothing**."
at the moment	/ət ðə 'məʊmənt/	im Augenblick	**At the moment** I'm staying in London.
park (n)★★	/pɑːk/	Park	Ben plays with his dog DJ in the **park**.
play (the guitar/ piano etc)★★★	/pleɪ (ðə gɪ'tɑː / pi'ænəʊ)/	spielen	Tomek **plays** the guitar.
read (v)★★★	/riːd/	lesen	What are you **reading** at the moment?
relax (v)★★	/rɪ'læks/	sich entspannen	He **relaxes** by playing with his dog.
short (adj)★★★	/ʃɔːt/	kurz	Gabi wears **short** skirts in the summer.
shorts (n pl)	/ʃɔːts/	kurze Hose; Shorts	Ben likes wearing **shorts**.
someone (pron)★★★	/'sʌmwʌn/	jemand	She tries to help **someone** every day.
special (adj)★★★	/'speʃəl/	besonders	"Is there something **special** you do every day?" "I try to help someone."
summer (n)★★★	/'sʌmə/	Sommer	What do you like wearing in **summer**?
stay (v)★★★	/steɪ/	wohnen	She's **staying** at the Royal Hotel.
sunshine (n)	/'sʌnʃaɪn/	Sonnenschein	**Sunshine** makes Gabi happy.
teacher (n)★★★	/'tiːtʃə/	Lehrer(in)	Ask your **teacher** for help.
think (v)★★★	/θɪŋk/	(nach)denken	That's a difficult question. Let me **think**.
truth (n)★★★	/truːθ/	Wahrheit	People who don't tell the **truth** make Tomek angry.
try (v)★★★	/traɪ/	versuchen	Gabi **tries** to help someone every day.
word (n)★★★	/wɜːd/	Wort	Gabi's favourite English **word** is "Sorry".

Inspiration Extra! (pp. 16–17)

All right.	/ɔːl 'raɪt/	Na schön.	"I haven't got a ticket." "**All right**. Then please leave the train."
birthday (n)★★	/'bɜːθdeɪ/	Geburtstag	When's your **birthday**?
buy (v)★★★	/baɪ/	kaufen	"I never **buy** a ticket." "Why not?"
continue (v)★★★	/kən'tɪnjuː/	…. weiter	The passenger **continues** reading.

dinner (n)★★★	/ˈdɪnə/	Abendessen	Does the passenger want seats for **dinner**?
food (n)★★★	/fuːd/	Essen	His favourite **food** is fish and chips.
Goodbye!★★★	/ɡʊdˈbaɪ/	Auf Wiedersehen!	This is my station. **Goodbye!**
leave (v)★★★	/liːv/	verlassen	Please **leave** the train.
move (v)★★★	/muːv/	sich bewegen	I can't leave the train – it's **moving**!
Pardon?	/ˈpɑːdən/	Bitte?	"What's your name?" "Tomek." "**Pardon?**" "Tomek."
passenger★★	/ˈpæsɪndʒə/	Fahrgast	The **passenger** is sitting on a train reading a newspaper.
TV programme (n)	/tiː ˈviː prəʊɡræm/	TV-Sendung	My favourite **TV programme** is Star Academy.
seat (n)★★★	/siːt/	(Sitz)platz	Do you want **seats** for dinner?
sell (v)★★★	/sel/	verkaufen	I'm not **selling** tickets. I want to see your ticket!
sir (form of address)	/sɜː/	mein Herr	I'm not selling tickets, **sir**!
sit (v)★★★	/sɪt/	sitzen	He is **sitting** on the train.
station (n)★★★	/ˈsteɪʃən/	Haltestelle	Please leave the train at the next **station**.
ticket (n)★★★	/ˈtɪkɪt/	Fahrkarte	You buy a **ticket** when you travel by train.
train (n)★★★	/treɪn/	Zug	The ticket inspector tells him to leave the **train**.
waiter (n)	/ˈweɪtə/	Kellner; Ober	The **waiter** says, "Seats for dinner?"
want (v)★★★	/wɒnt/	wollen	He doesn't **want** to buy a ticket.
website (n)	/ˈwebsaɪt/	Internet-Adresse	Our **website** address is: www.macmillanenglish.com.

Culture: Welcome to London (pp. 18–19)

also (adv)★★★	/ˈɔːlsəʊ/	auch	There are shops in Covent Garden and **also** cafés and restaurants.
aquarium (n)	/əˈkweəriəm/	Aquarium	An **aquarium** is a place where you can see unusual fish.
bell (n)★★	/bel/	Glocke	Big Ben is the name of a **bell** in the clock tower of the Houses of Parliament.
big (adj)★★★	/bɪɡ/	groß	Covent Garden was once London's **biggest** flower, fruit and vegetable market.
big wheel (n)	/bɪɡ ˈwiːl/	Riesenrad	The **big wheel** in the centre of London is called the London Eye.
boat (n)★★★	/bəʊt/	Boot	Take a sightseeing **boat** along Regent's Canal.
canal (n)	/kəˈnæl/	Kanal	The **canal** goes past Regent's Park and London Zoo.
capsule (n)	/ˈkæpsjuːl/	Kapsel; Kabine	The London Eye has 32 **capsules** which carry 25 passengers each.
careful (adj)★★★	/ˈkeəfəl/	vorsichtig	Be **careful**! There are lots of pickpockets here.
cathedral (n)	/kəˈθiːdrəl/	Kathedrale	St Paul's is the fifth **cathedral** on the site.
centre (n)★★★	/ˈsentə/	Zentrum	Which famous tourist attraction is in the exact **centre** of London?

Christmas Day (n)	/krɪsməs 'deɪ/	erster Weihnachtstag	Madame Tussaud's is open every day of the year except **Christmas Day**.
church (n)★★★	/tʃɜːtʃ/	Kirche	St Paul's Cathedral is the most famous **church** in London.
city (n)★★★	/'sɪti/	City; Stadt	You can look out over the **city** from the top of The Monument.
climb (v)★★★	/klaɪm/	hinaufsteigen	**Climb** to the top of the 300-year-old monument for a fabulous view of London.
clock (n)★★★	/klɒk/	Uhr	Big Ben is actually the name of a bell not a **clock**.
clock tower (n)	/klɒk taʊə/	Uhr(en)turm	Big Ben is in the **clock tower** of the Houses of Parliament.
column (n)★★	/kɒləm/	Säule	The Monument is a 61.5-metre tall **column**.
double-decker bus (n)	/ˌdʌbl dekə 'bʌs/	Doppeldecker	London is famous for its red **double-decker buses**.
equal to★★★	/iːkwəl tə/	gleich	The aquarium uses salt **equal to** the weight of nine double-decker buses.
exact (adj)★	/ɪgˈzækt/	genau	"Where is the London Eye?" "In the **exact** centre of London."
exactly (adv)★★★	/ɪgˈzæktli/	genau	The Monument is **exactly** 61.5 metres tall.
exciting (adj)★★	/ɪkˈsaɪtɪŋ/	aufregend	You can buy lots of **exciting** things at Camden Market.
face to face	/ˌfeɪs tə 'feɪs/	hautnah; Auge in Auge	Meet sharks **face to face** at the London Aquarium!
famous (adj)★★★	/ˈfeɪməs/	berühmt	There are lots of models of **famous** people at Madame Tussaud's.
film character (n)	/fɪlm kærɪktə/	Filmfigur	You can see models of **film** stars and **characters**.
film star (n)	/fɪlm stɑː/	Filmstar	Who's your favourite **film star**?
fire (n)★★★	/faɪə/	Brand; Feuer	The **fire** started in 1666.
fruit (n)★★★	/fruːt/	Obst	Covent Garden was once a **fruit** and vegetable market.
fun (n)★★	/fʌn/	Spaß	The London Eye is new and it's **fun**.
high (adj)★★★	/haɪ/	hoch	How **high** is the tower of the Houses of Parliament?
history (n)★★★	/ˈhɪstəri/	Geschichte	You can sit in the back of a taxi and "travel" through London's **history** in five minutes.
in fact	/ɪn 'fækt/	in Wirklichkeit	**In fact**, Big Ben is really the name of one of the clock's bells.
interesting (adj)★★★	/ˈɪntrəstɪŋ/	interessant	People who like fish find the London Aquarium very **interesting**.
king (n)★★★	/kɪŋ/	König	You can see models of **kings** and queens in Madame Tussaud's.
look down	/lʊk 'daʊn/	hinunterschauen	**Look down** on London as you ride on the London Eye.
look out	/lʊk 'aʊt/	hinausschauen	**Look out** over London from the top of The Monument.
lots of★★★	/lɒts əv/	viele; eine Menge	**Lots of** tourists visit London each year.
market (n)★★	/ˈmɑːkɪt/	Markt	Camden **Market** sells all sorts of things including clothes and records.
miss (v)★★★	/mɪs/	verpassen	Don't **miss** the Chamber of Horrors!
model (n)★★★	/mɒdl/	Figur	Madame Tussaud's has lots of **models** of famous people.
monument (n)	/ˈmɒnjʊmənt/	Denkmal	Visit London's famous **monuments** and tourist attractions.

museum (n)★★★	/mjuːˈziəm/	Museum	The British **Museum** is the most visited tourist attraction in the city.
new (adj)★★★	/njuː/	neu	One of London's **newest** tourist attractions is the London Eye.
open (adj)★★★	/ˈəʊpn/	offen; auf	The aquarium is **open** from 10am–6pm.
own (adj)★★★	/əʊn/	eigen	It makes its **own** seawater.
past (prep)★★★	/pɑːst/	an … vorbei	The sightseeing boat goes **past** Regent's Park.
place (n)★★★	/pleɪs/	Ort	An aquarium is a **place** where you can see unusual fish.
popular (adj)★★★	/ˈpɒpjələ/	beliebt	The British Museum is London's second most **popular** tourist attraction.
queen (n)★★★	/kwiːn/	Königin	You can see models of kings and **queens** in Madame Tussaud's.
real (adj)★★★	/riːl/	echt	Sit in the back of a **real** black taxi and travel through London's history.
rebuild (v)	/riːˈbɪld/	wiederaufbauen	St Paul's Cathedral was **rebuilt** after the Great Fire of London.
record (n)★★★	/ˈrekɔːd/	Schallplatte	You can buy great **records** at Camden Market.
ride (n)★	/raɪd/	Reise	Sit in the back of a taxi and have a time **ride** through London.
ride (v)★★	/raɪd/	fahren	Lots of people **ride** on the London Eye each year.
salt (n)★	/sɒlt/	Salz	The aquarium uses **salt** to makes its own seawater.
seawater (n)	/ˈsiːwɔːtə/	Meereswasser	**Seawater** contains lots of salt.
shark (n)	/ʃɑːk/	Hai(fisch)	**Sharks** are very dangerous animals that live in the sea.
shopping (n)★★	/ˈʃɒpɪŋ/	Einkaufen; Shopping	Camden Market and Covent Garden are great places for **shopping**.
site (n)★★★	/saɪt/	Stelle	The London Eye is built on a **site** in the exact centre of London.
sky (n)★★★	/skaɪ/	Himmel	Visit The Monument and the London Eye and see London from the **sky**!
slow (adj)★★★	/sləʊ/	langsam	It's the **slowest** big wheel in the world.
start (v)★★★	/stɑːt/	ausbrechen; beginnen	"When did the Great Fire of London **start**?" "In 1666."
stone (n)★★★	/stəʊn/	Stein	The Monument is 61.5 metres tall and made of **stone**.
street theatre (n)	/ˈstriːt ˌθɪətə/	Straßentheater	You can usually see buskers and **street theatre** in Covent Garden.
tall (adj)★★★	/tɔːl/	hoch	The column is exactly 61.5 metres **tall**.
tour (n)★★	/tʊə/	Rundreise	Take a sightseeing **tour** along Regent's Canal.
tourist attraction (n)	/ˈtʊərɪst əˌtrækʃən/	Touristenattraktion	On p. 18 you can read about nine **tourist attractions** in London.
travel (v)★★★	/ˈtrævəl/	fahren	**Travel** on a double-decker bus in London!
unusual (adj)★★	/ʌnˈjuːʒʊəl/	ungewöhnlich	There are some very **unusual** fish at the London Aquarium.
vegetable (n)★★★	/ˈvedʒtəbəl/	Gemüse	Covent Garden was once a fruit and **vegetable** market.
view (n)★★★	/vjuː/	Ausblick	You can get good **views** of London from The London Eye and The Monument.
weigh (v)★★	/weɪ/	wiegen	Big Ben is the name of one of the clock's bells and **weighs** over 13 tonnes.
weight (n)★★★	/weɪt/	Gewicht	The aquarium uses salt equal to the **weight** of nine double-decker buses.

whisper (v)★	/wɪspə/	flüstern	In the Whispering Gallery you can hear people **whisper** 30 metres away.
world (n)★★★	/wɜːld/	Welt	London is one of the most interesting cities in the **world**.
zoo (n)	/zuː/	Zoo	A **zoo** is a place where people go to see unusual animals.

Unit 2

1 Europe's best street party (pp. 20–21)

all-night (adj)	/ɔːl 'raɪt/	durch die ganze Nacht	**All-night** dances take place with loud music.
amazing (adj)★	/əˈmeɪzɪŋ/	erstaunlich	The bands at Notting Hill carnival wear **amazing** colourful costumes.
ball (n)★★★	/bɔːl/	Ball	The carnival **balls** in Rio are enormous dances with loud music.
band (n)★★★	/bænd/	Band; Kapelle	**Bands** parade through the streets playing loud music.
carnival (n)	/kɑːnɪvəl/	Karneval	The **carnival** in Rio is longer than the Notting Hill carnival.
celebrate (v)★★	/seləbreɪt/	feiern	In Brazil people **celebrate** carnival in February or March.
choose (v)★★★	/tʃuːz/	wählen	Judges **choose** the best dancers.
cold (adj)★★★	/kəʊld/	kalt	In winter the weather is often very **cold**.
colourful (adj)	/kʌləfəl/	farbenprächtig	People in the parades wear amazing **colourful** costumes.
cosmopolitan (adj)	/kɒzməˈpɒlɪtən/	kosmopolitisch	At carnival time Notting Hill becomes **cosmopolitan**, with visitors from all over the world.
costume (n)	/kɒstʃuːm/	Kostüm	The dancers in Rio wear amazing **costumes**.
country (n)★★★	/kʌntri/	Land	Do you have carnivals in your **country**?
dancer (n)	/dɑːnsə/	Tänzer(in)	**Dancers** wear the most amazing costumes.
drummer (n)	/drʌmə/	Trommler; Schlagzeuger	Some parades have 600 to 800 **drummers**.
dry (adj)★★★	/draɪ/	trocken	The climate here is **dry**, with very little rain.
at the end of	/ət ðiː 'end əv/	(am) Ende	Over a million people go to the carnival **at the end of** August.
exotic (adj)	/ɪɡˈzɒtɪk/	exotisch	You can buy **exotic** food from all over the world.
festival (n)	/festɪvəl/	Fest(spiel)	A carnival is a type of **festival**.
follow (v)★★★	/fɒləʊ/	folgen	People dance and **follow** the bands.
foreign (adj)★★★	/fɒrɪn/	ausländisch	About 300,000 **foreign** visitors go to Rio every year.
full of★★★	/fʊl əv/	voller	The streets are **full of** people at carnival time.
giant (adj)	/dʒaɪənt/	riesig	The **giant** samba stadium holds 90,000 people.
How long?	/haʊ 'lɒŋ/	Wie lange?	"**How long** does the carnival last?" "Two days."

How many?	/haʊ ˈmeni/	Wie viele?	**"How many** bands are there at Notting Hill?" "More than fifty."
hungry (adj)★	/ˈhʌŋgri/	hungrig	When you get **hungry** you can buy exotic food from stalls.
including (prep)★★★	/ɪŋˈkluːdɪŋ/	einschließlich	Millions of people go to Rio **including** 300,000 foreign visitors.
judge (n)★★	/dʒʌdʒ/	Preisrichter	**Judges** choose the best dancers.
kind★★★	/kaɪnd/	Art	What **kind** of music do they play?
large (adj)★★★	/lɑːdʒ/	groß	It's the **largest** carnival in Europe.
last (v)★★★	/lɑːst/	dauern	"How long does the Notting Hill carnival **last**?" "Two days."
long (adj)★★★	/lɒŋ/	lang	The Rio carnival is quite **long** – it lasts four days.
loud (adj)★★	/laʊd/	laut	People dance to **loud** music.
money (n)★★★	/ˈmʌni/	Geld	You need a lot of **money** because hotels and taxis cost four times as much as usual.
nice (adj)★★★	/naɪs/	nett	The people here are **nice** and friendly.
noisy (adj)★	/ˈnɔɪzi/	laut(stark)	Notting Hill is usually quiet but at carnival time it's very **noisy**.
non-stop (adj)	/nɒn stɒp/	non-stop; pausenlos	**Non-stop** loud music plays through the night.
old (adj)★★★	/əʊld/	alt	Is Granada the **oldest** city in Spain?
parade (n)	/pəˈreɪd/	Parade; Umzug	Some **parades** have thousands of dancers.
parade (v)	/pəˈreɪd/	vorbeimarschieren	More than fifty bands **parade** through the streets.
quiet (adj)★★★	/ˈkwaɪət/	ruhig	'**Quiet**' means the opposite of 'loud' or 'noisy'.
reggae (n)	/ˈregeɪ/	Reggae	**Reggae** music comes from the Caribbean.
region (n)★★★	/ˈriːdʒən/	Region; Gebiet	Every **region** in Brazil has its own festival.
say (v)★★★	/seɪ/	sagen	The people of Rio **say** their carnival is the best.
show (n)★★★	/ʃəʊ/	Show	People call Notting Hill carnival 'The Greatest **Show** on Earth'.
size (n)★★★	/saɪz/	Größe	Madrid is the biggest city in Spain in **size**.
small (adj)★★★	/smɔːl/	klein	The carnival in Notting Hill is **smaller** than the one in Rio.
smart (adj)★	/smɑːt/	schick; fein	Notting Hill is a **smart**, expensive part of London.
sound system (n)	/ˈsaʊnd sɪstəm/	Tonanlage; Audio-System	**Sound systems** play reggae and other kinds of music.
spectacular (adj)	/spekˈtækjʊlə/	spektakulär; atemberaubend	It's the biggest, most **spectacular** carnival in the world!
stage (n)★★★	/steɪdʒ/	Bühne	There are three **stages** where bands play.
stall (n)	/stɔːl/	Stand	**Stalls** sell exotic food from all over the world.
street (n)★★★	/striːt/	Straße	Parades in the **streets** last ten to twelve hours.
street party (n)	/striːt pɑːti/	Straßenfest	People call Notting Hill carnival Europe's best **street party**!
warm (adj)★★★	/wɔːm/	warm	Most people prefer **warm**, dry weather.
weather (n)★★★	/ˈweðə/	Wetter	In summer the **weather** is nice and warm.

wet (adj)★★★	/wet/	nass; feucht	It's raining – everything's **wet**!
well-known (adj)	/ˌwel ˈnəʊn/	(sehr) bekannt	Rio is **well-known** for its carnival.

2 We should stay together (pp. 22–3)

address (n)★★★	/əˈdres/	Adresse; Anschrift	"What's your **address**?" "6 Radley Avenue, Chester."
agree (with) (v)★★★	/əˈgriː (wɪð)/	der gleichen Meinung sein	Carol doesn't **agree** with Greg.
answer (v)★★★	/ˈɑːnsə/	rangehen	What do you say when you **answer** the telephone?
arrive (v)★★★	/əˈraɪv/	da sein; ankommen	What time should we **arrive**?
ask (v)★★★	/ɑːsk/	bitten	Greg **asks** the others to meet him in half an hour.
bank (n)★★★	/bæŋk/	Bank	I want to change some money. Where's the **bank**?
behind (prep)★★★	/bɪˈhaɪnd/	hinter	Sally is standing **behind** Ben.
between (prep)★★★	/bɪˈtwiːn/	zwischen	Gabi is standing **between** Tomek and Laura.
book (v)★	/bʊk/	buchen	I want to **book** a flight to Frankfurt.
bookshop (n)	/ˈbʊkʃɒp/	Buchhandlung	Is there a **bookshop** where I can buy some magazines?
bread (n)★★★	/bred/	Brot	Don't forget to buy **bread** at the supermarket.
Bye! (interj)★	/baɪ/	Tschüss	See you later. **Bye!**
carry (v)★★★	/ˈkæri/	mit sich tragen	Don't **carry** lots of money.
change some money	/tʃeɪndʒ sʌm ˈmʌni/	Geld wechseln	You can **change some money** at the bank or the travel agency.
cheek (n)★★	/tʃiːk/	Wange; Backe	In Britain it's less common for people to kiss each other on the **cheek**.
chemist's (n)	/ˈkemɪsts/	Apotheke(r)	You can buy medicine at a **chemist's**.
children (n pl)★★★	/ˈtʃɪldrən/	Kinder	It's important to look after **children**.
come back (phr v)	/kʌm ˈbæk/	zurückkommen	Carol, Ben, **come back**!
crowd (n)★★★	/kraʊd/	(Menschen)menge	Walk in the same direction as the **crowd**.
cup (of coffee/tea) (n)★★★	/kʌp əv ˈkɒfi/tiː/	Tasse	"How much is a **cup** of coffee?" "80p."
direction (n)★★★	/dɪˈrekʃən, daɪˈrekʃən/	Richtung	Everyone was walking in the same **direction**.
early (adv)★★★	/ˈɜːli/	früh(zeitig)	We arrived at their house **early**.
eat (v)★★★	/iːt/	essen	Don't start **eating** first when you're a guest at someone's house.
everything (pron)★★★	/ˈevriθɪŋ/	alles	Try to eat **everything** on your plate.
find (v)★★★	/faɪnd/	finden	You can **find** all kinds of newspapers and magazines at the newsagent's.
flight (n)★★★	/flaɪt/	Flug	You can book **flights** at a travel agency.
flower shop (n)	/ˈflaʊə ʃɒp/	Blumenladen	The **flower shop** is selling some beautiful flowers.
in front of (prep)	/ɪn ˈfrʌnt əv/	vor	You shouldn't jump **in front of** a band.
get (v)★★★	/get/	bekommen	"Where can I **get** a magazine?" "At the newsagent's."

go away (phr v)	/gəʊ əˈweɪ/	weggehen	Don't **go away** like that!
guest (n)★★	/gest/	Gast	How many **guests** came to the party?
haircut (n)	/ˈheəkʌt/	Haarschnitt; Frisur; Haare schneiden lassen	If you need a **haircut** go to the hairdresser's.
hairdresser's (n)	/ˈheədresəz/	Friseur	I'm going to the **hairdresser's** for a haircut.
immediately (adv)★★★	/ɪˈmiːdɪətli/	sofort	Come here **immediately**!
inside (prep)★★★	/ɪnˈsaɪd/	innerhalb; in ... drin	There are flowers outside the flower shop and **inside** it there are even more.
jewellery (n)★★	/ˈdʒʊəlri/	Schmuck	Bangles are a type of **jewellery**.
jump (v)★★★	/dʒʌmp/	springen	Don't **jump** in front of a band – follow it.
kiss (v)★	/kɪs/	küssen	Do people **kiss** each other on the cheek to say 'hello' in your country?
look after (phr v)	/lʊk ˈɑːftə/	aufpassen auf	It's Greg's job to **look after** everyone.
lost (adj)★	/lɒst/	verloren	It's easy to get **lost** during a big carnival.
magazine (n)★★	/mæɡəˈziːn/	Zeitschrift; Magazin	Do you prefer reading books or **magazines**?
meal (n)★★★	/miːl/	Essen	We're going to their house for a **meal**.
medicine (n)★★	/ˈmedsən/	Medizin; Medikament; Arzneimittel	I'm going to the chemist's to buy some **medicine**.
near (prep)★★★	/nɪə/	neben; in der Nähe von	Tomek is standing **near** Greg.
newsagent's (n)	/ˈnjuːzeɪdʒənts/	Zeitungshändler	The **newsagent's** sells lots of different newspapers.
next to (prep)★★★	/ˈneks tə/	neben	Carol, Pedro and Jack are dancing **next to** the band.
on your own	/ɒn jɔːr ˈəʊn/	allein	You shouldn't go off **on your own**. It isn't safe.
once (adv)★★★	/wʌns/	einmal	Do you kiss your friends on the cheek **once** or twice?
open (v)★★★	/ˈəʊpn/	öffnen; aufmachen	Can I **open** my present?
opposite (prep)★	/ˈɒpəzɪt/	gegenüber	The YTV stage is **opposite** the cinema.
outside (prep)★★★	/aʊtˈsaɪd/	draußen vor	**Outside** the flower shop are lots of flowers.
over (prep)★★★	/ˈəʊvə/	über	The travel agency is **over** the café.
plate (n)★★★	/pleɪt/	Teller	There's too much food on my **plate**.
police station (n)	/pəˈliːs steɪʃən/	Polizeiwache	If you get lost you can go to the **police station** and ask for directions.
post office (n)	/ˈpəʊst ɒfɪs/	Postamt	You can buy stamps at the **post office**.
present (n)★★★	/ˈprezənt/	Geschenk	"Here's a **present** for you." "Thank you."
questionnaire (n)	/kwestʃəˈneə/	Fragebogen	There are five questions in the YTV **questionnaire**.
the rest (of you) (n)★★★	/ðə ˈrest (əv juː)/	die anderen	Listen to me, **the rest** of you.
safe (adj)★★★	/seɪf/	sicher; ungefährlich	It isn't **safe** to go off on your own.

same (adj)★★★	/seɪm/	gleich	You should all walk in the **same** direction.
shake hands	/ʃeɪk ˈhændz/	die Hände schütteln	When you meet someone's parents in Britain you should **shake hands**.
should (v)★★★	/ʃʊd/	sollten	You **should** tell me where you're going. I'm looking after you.
sign (n)★★★	/saɪn/	Schild	On the **sign** it says: 'Don't walk on the grass.'
stamp (n)★★	/stæmp/	Briefmarke	I need a **stamp** for this postcard.
supermarket (n)★	/ˈsuːpəmɑːkɪt/	Supermarkt	Let's buy some bread at the **supermarket**.
thank you★★★	/ˈθæŋk juː/	Danke schön	"Here's a present for you." "**Thank you**."
together (adv)★★★	/təˈɡeðə/	zusammen	It's easy to get lost here – let's stay **together**.
travel agency (n)	/ˈtrævəl eɪdʒənsi/	Reisebüro	If you want to book a flight go to the **travel agency**.
twice (adv)★★★	/twaɪs/	zweimal	Do you kiss your friends on the cheek once or **twice**?
under (prep)★★★	/ˈʌndə/	unter	It's raining. Stand **under** my umbrella.
wait (for) (v)★★★	/weɪt (tə)/	warten	Please **wait** for ten minutes.
walk (v)★★★	/wɔːk/	zu Fuß gehen	Let's **walk** to the station.

3 I love going to festivals (pp. 24–5)

bad at★★★	/bæd æt/	schlecht in	We're not brilliant at English but we're not **bad at** it.
bossy (adj)	/ˈbɒsi/	kommandiert gerne rum	Carol thinks Greg is **bossy**.
dance (v)★★★	/dɑːns/	tanzen	What type of music do you like **dancing** to?
enjoy (v)★★★	/ɪnˈdʒɔɪ/	gerne machen; einem Spaß machen	What kind of things do you **enjoy** doing?
fantastic (adj)	/fænˈtæstɪk/	fantastisch	This is a **fantastic** carnival!
good at★★★	/ɡʊd æt/	gut können	Ben tells Carol she is really **good at** dancing.
hate (v)★★★	/heɪt/	hassen	Some people **hate** large crowds.
heavy metal (n)	/hevi ˈmetəl/	Heavymetal	**Heavy metal** is a kind of very loud rock music.
house (n)★★★	/haʊs/	House	**House** is a type of popular fast dance music.
interested (in) (adj)★★★	/ˈɪntrəstɪd (ɪn)/	sich interessieren für	Paula is **interested** in talking to the competition winners.
jazz (n)	/dʒæz/	Jazz	Which do you prefer – **jazz** or rap?
lose (v)★★★	/luːz/	verlieren	Try not to **lose** anything.
love (v)★★★	/lʌv/	lieben; etwas sehr gerne tun	They **love** going to festivals.
notice (v)★★★	/ˈnəʊtɪs/	bemerken	People don't **notice** you in a crowd.
pop (n)★	/pɒp/	Pop(musik)	I prefer **pop** to classical.
punk (n)	/pʌŋk/	Punk	**Punk** is a kind of loud, fast rock music.
rap (n)	/ræp/	Rap	Eminem is a famous **rap** artist.

rock (n)★★★	/rɒk/	Rock	My hobbies are computer games and listening to **rock**.
rude (to) (adj)★	/ruːd (tə)/	grob; unhöflich	"You were **rude** to Greg." "Well, he's bossy."
soul (n)★	/səʊl/	Soul	Which famous **soul** singers do you know?
can't stand	/kɑːnt 'stænd/	nicht aushalten können	Carol **can't stand** waiting a long time for people.
stupid (adj)★★	/'stjuːpɪd/	blöd	I feel **stupid** dancing on my own.
techno (n)	/'teknəʊ/	Techno	**Techno** music uses electronic instruments and synthesizers.
use (v)★★★	/juːz/	benutzen; mit.... umgehen	He's teaching his mum how to **use** a computer.
world (n)★★★	/wɜːld/	aus aller Welt; international	The shop sells a lot of **world** music – from Africa, South America, Europe and Asia.

4 Integrated Skills: Celebrations (pp. 26–7)

arrival (n)★★	/ə'raɪvəl/	Ankunft	Italy celebrates the **arrival** of the New Year with fireworks.
beach (n)★★	/biːtʃ/	Strand	They go down to the **beach** at midnight and jump over the waves.
bring (v)★★★	/brɪŋ/	bringen	People in Brazil think that white clothes **bring** good luck.
burn (v)★★★	/bɜːn/	verbrennen	Some people write their wishes in a letter and then **burn** it.
candle (n)	/'kændəl/	Kerze	If it's too dark, light a **candle**.
celebration (n)★★★	/selə'breɪʃən/	Feier(lichkeiten)	New Year **celebrations** last 15 days in China.
champagne (n)	/ʃæm'peɪn/	Champagner; Sekt	People often drink **champagne** to celebrate something.
dragon (n)	/'drægən/	Drache	There are **dragon** parades for the Chinese New Year.
drink (v)★★★	/drɪŋk/	trinken	Everyone **drinks** sake, a type of rice wine.
envelope (n)★★★	/'envələʊp/	Kuvert; Briefumschlag	Children in Japan get red **envelopes** with money inside.
fireworks (n pl)	/'faɪəwɜːks/	Feuerwerk	Many European countries celebrate the New Year with **fireworks**.
game (n)★★★	/geɪm/	Spiel	In Thailand people play **games** with water.
good luck	/gʊd 'lʌk/	Glück	Do you think that wearing white clothes brings **good luck**?
grape (n)	/greɪp/	Traube	When they hear the bells they eat a **grape**.
greetings card (n)	/'griːtɪŋz kɑːd/	Grußkarte	A lot of people send **greetings cards** at New Year.
house (n)★★★	/haʊs/	Haus	People who want to travel in the New Year carry a suitcase round the **house**!
lentils (n pl)	/'lentəlz/	Linse	**Lentils** are a type of small round bean, often eaten in soup.
light (v)★★	/laɪt/	anzünden	Some people **light** candles to celebrate the New Year.
lion (n)	/'laɪən/	Löwe	A **lion** is a very big wild animal that we call 'King of the Jungle".

make a wish	/meɪk ə 'wɪʃ/	sich etwas wünschen	A lot of people **make wishes** at the New Year.
member (n)★★★	/'membə/	Mitglied	Each family **member** gets a candle.
noodles (n pl)	/'nuːdəlz/	Nudeln	On 31st December the Japanese eat special **noodles**.
New Year	/ˌnjuː 'jɪə/	Neujahr	The article is about how people celebrate **New Year** in different parts of the world.
New Year's Eve	/ˌnjuː jɪəz 'iːv/	Silvester	How do you celebrate **New Year's Eve** in your country?
party (n)★★★	/'pɑːti/	Party; Feier	There are always lots of **parties** at New Year.
rice (n)★	/raɪs/	Reis	Sake is a type of wine made from **rice**.
ring (v)★★★	/rɪŋ/	läuten	The bells **ring** 108 times.
send (v)★★★	/send/	schicken; senden	A lot of people **send** greetings cards.
soup (n)★	/suːp/	Suppe	The Japanese drink sake and eat a special kind of **soup**.
start (n)★★★	/stɑːt/	Anfang	The **start** of the Chinese New Year is in January or February.
suitcase (n)	/'suːtkeɪs/	Koffer	You put your clothes in a **suitcase** when you are travelling.
throw (v)★★★	/θrəʊ/	werfen	People **throw** flowers into the sea and make wishes.
tradition (n)★★★	/trə'dɪʃən/	Tradition	One **tradition** in Italy is to put a candle in the window for each member of the family.
traditional (adj)★★★	/trə'dɪʃnəl/	traditionell	The **traditional** Japanese rice wine is called sake.
underwear (n)	/'ʌndəweə/	Unterwäsche	In Venezuela people wear yellow **underwear** for good luck!
water (n)★★★	/'wɔːtə/	Wasser	On 'Song Klarn Day' in Thailand people throw **water** over each other!
wave (n)★★	/weɪv/	Welle	They jump over the **waves** in the sea seven times.
window (n)★★★	/'wɪndəʊ/	Fenster	They put a candle in the **window** for each family member.
wine (n)★★★	/waɪn/	Wein	Sake is a kind of **wine** made from rice.

Inspiration *Extra!* (pp. 28–9)

anything (pron)★★★	/'enɪθɪŋ/	etwas	Is there **anything** you'd like to ask?
cost (v)★★★	/kɒst/	kosten	How much do the tickets **cost**?
get up (phr v)	/get 'ʌp/	aufstehen	He usually **gets up** early – at 7.00.
homework (n)★	/'həʊmwɜːk/	Hausaufgaben	I hate doing **homework**!
perform (v)★★★	/pə'fɔːm/	auftreten; spielen	Who is **performing** at the concert?
poem (n)★	/'pəʊɪm/	Gedicht	Do you enjoy writing **poems**?

Review Units 1–2 (pp. 30–31)

bonfire (n)	/ˈbɒnfaɪə/	großes (Lager)feuer	People celebrate Guy Fawkes' Night on 5th November with **bonfires** and fireworks.
carriage (n)	/ˈkærɪdʒ/	Kutsche	The Queen rides in an open **carriage** to see 'The Trooping of the Colour'.
central (adj)★★★	/ˈsentrəl/	zentral; im ... Zentrum	Buckingham Palace is in **central** London.
Christmas tree (n)	/ˈkrɪsməs triː/	Weihnachtsbaum	At Christmas there is a huge **Christmas tree** in Trafalgar Square.
Easter (n)	/ˈiːstə/	Ostern	Every year there is a parade at **Easter** in Battersea Park.
enough (adj)★★★	/ɪˈnʌf/	genug	Make sure you've got **enough** money for a taxi.
failure (n)★★★	/ˈfeɪljə/	Versagen	People celebrate Guy Fawkes' **failure** to kill the king.
forget (v)★★★	/fəˈget/	vergessen	Don't **forget** to check the times of the last trains and buses.
Hindu (adj)	/ˈhɪnduː/	Hindu-	Diwali is the **Hindu** festival of lights.
Hindu (n)	/ˈhɪnduː/	Hindu	Diwali is celebrated by **Hindus**.
lift (n)★	/lɪft/	Mitfahrgelegenheit	Never accept a **lift** from a stranger.
mobile (phone) (n)	/ˈməʊbaɪl (fəʊn)/	Handy	Always carry a **mobile** or a phone card.
phone card (n)	/ˈfəʊn kɑːd/	Telefonkarte	You can use a public phone if you have a **phone card**.
show (v)★★★	/ʃəʊ/	zeigen	The Notting Hill carnival **shows** that London is very cosmopolitan.
sing (v)★★★	/sɪŋ/	singen	A busker plays music and often **sings** in the street.
stranger (n)★	/ˈstreɪndʒə/	Fremde(r); Unbekannte(r)	Don't accept lifts from **strangers** or get into a stranger's car.

Unit 3

1 The fire started at a baker's (pp. 32–3)

after (prep)★★★	/ˈɑːftə/	nach	**After** many weeks of hot weather everything was very dry.
asleep (adj)★★	/əˈsliːp/	eingeschlafen; sich schlafen gelegt	People were **asleep** when the Great Fire started.
baker's (n)	/ˈbeɪkəz/	Bäckerei	The fire started at a **baker's** near London Bridge.
ball-point pen (n)	/ˌbɔːl pɔɪnt ˈpen/	Kugelschreiber	In English we also call a **ball-point pen** a 'biro', after the name of the man who invented it.
become (v)★★★	/bɪˈkʌm/	werden	London **became** the most important town in Britain.
be born (v)	/bi ˈbɔːn/	geboren sein/werden	I **was born** in 1990.
brandy (n)	/ˈbrændi/	Weinbrand	**Brandy** is a strong alcoholic drink.

bridge (n)★★	/brɪdʒ/	Brücke	The Millennium **Bridge** is the newest bridge over the Thames.
build (v)★★★	/bɪld/	bauen	They **built** a town called Londinium – it's now called London.
building (n)★★★	/ˈbɪldɪŋ/	Gebäude	The Great Fire destroyed many **buildings**.
bury (v)★	/ˈberi/	begraben	He didn't want the fire to destroy his cheese and wine so he **buried** them in his garden!
butter (n)★★	/ˈbʌtə/	Butter	I usually have bread and **butter** for breakfast.
by (prep)★★★	/baɪ/	bis	**By** the evening of Wednesday, 5th September, there weren't many buildings left.
century (n)★★★	/ˈsentʃʊri/	Jahrhundert	The Romans came to Britain in the first **century** AD.
cheese (n)★★	/tʃiːz/	Käse	We had a simple meal of **cheese** and bread.
close (adj)★★★	/kləʊs/	nah	At 4 am on Monday the fire was much **closer**.
cross (v)★★★	/krɒs/	überqueren	Luckily the fire didn't **cross** the river.
describe (v)★★★	/dɪsˈkraɪb/	beschreiben	Pepys **described** many important events in his diary.
design (v)★★★	/dɪˈzaɪn/	entwerfen	A man called Laszlo Biró **designed** the first ball-point pen.
destroy (v)★★★	/dɪsˈtrɔɪ/	zerstören	In 1666 the Great Fire of London **destroyed** most of the city.
diary (n)★★	/ˈdaɪəri/	Tagebuch	Samuel Pepys is the author of a famous **diary**.
die (v)★★★	/daɪ/	sterben	Luckily only four people **died** in the fire.
escape (v)★★	/ɪsˈkeɪp/	flüchten	Most people **escaped** to the fields outside the city.
event (n)★★★	/ɪˈvent/	Ereignisse	His diary describes many important **events** and is very interesting.
eye (n)★★★	/aɪ/	Auge	He stopped writing when his **eyes** became too bad.
field (n)★★★	/fiːld/	Feld	A **field** is an area of land in the countryside where animals eat or where food grows.
on fire	/ɒn ˈfaɪə/	brennen	Houses were **on fire** at the end of London Bridge.
flame (n)★	/fleɪm/	Flamme	The **flames** quickly reached tall buildings full of inflammable things.
for (prep)★★★	/fɔː/	...lang	The fire burnt **for** four days.
hot (adj)★★★	/hɒt/	heiß	Everything was very dry after many weeks of **hot** weather.
in (prep)★★★	/ɪn/	im Jahre	Was Pepys born **in** 1633?
inflammable (adj)	/ɪnˈflæməbəl/	entzündbar; feuergefährlich	Something that is **inflammable** burns very easily.
invent (v)★★	/ɪnˈvent/	erfinden	Who **invented** the Walkman?
luckily (adv)	/ˈlʌkɪli/	glücklicherweise	**Luckily** the fire didn't cross the river.
marry (v)★★	/ˈmæri/	heiraten	What year did they **marry**?
nightclothes (n pl)	/ˈnaɪtkləʊðz/	Nachthemd; Nachtwäsche	Pepys and his wife left their home in their **nightclothes**.
oil (n)★★★	/ɔɪl/	Öl	**Oil** is a black or brown liquid that burns easily.

on (prep)★★★	/ɒn/	an	The Great Fire started **on** Sunday 2nd September, 1666.
pack (v)★	/pæk/	packen	When he saw the fire Pepys went home and started to **pack**.
phone call (n)	/ˈfəʊn kɔːl/	(telefonischer) Anruf	Who made the first **phone call**?
print (v)★★	/prɪnt/	drucken	William Caxton **printed** the first book in English.
rain (n)★★★	/reɪn/	Regen	There had been no **rain** and everything was very dry.
reach (v)★★★	/riːtʃ/	erreichen	The fire **reached** tall buildings full of inflammable things.
return (v)★★★	/rɪˈtɜːn/	zurückkehren	Pepys **returned** later in the day to bury cheese and wine in his garden!
smoke (n)★★	/sməʊk/	Rauch	The sky was full of flames and **smoke**.
space (n)★★★	/speɪs/	Weltraum	Yuri Gagarin was the first person to travel in **space**.
study (v)★★★	/ˈstʌdi/	studieren	Which university did he **study** at?
then (adv)★★★	/ðen/	zu dem Zeitpunkt	He saw houses on fire on Sunday morning but the fire wasn't near his house **then**.
Walkman (n)	/ˈwɔːkmən/	Walkman	She's listening to a CD on her **Walkman**.
wind (n)★★★	/wɪnd/	Wind	The **wind** carried the flames to the River Thames.
wine (n)★★★	/waɪn/	Wein	I prefer red **wine** to white wine.

2 Did you have fun? (pp. 34–5)

architect (n)	/ˈɑːkɪtekt/	Architekt	**Architects** design buildings.
between (prep)★★★	/bɪˈtwiːn/	zwischen	What did the group do **between** 10.45 and 11.45?
brilliant (adj)★	/ˈbrɪljənt/	brillant; großartig	We went to the Globe Theatre – it was **brilliant**!
burn down (phr v)	/bɜːn ˈdaʊn/	niederbrennen	St Paul's Cathedral **burnt down** in 1666 during the fire.
come down (phr v)	/kʌm ˈdaʊn/	herunterkommen	We were exhausted when we **came down**!
complete (adj)★★★	/kəmˈpliːt/	vollständig	In what year was the cathedral **complete**?
exhausted (adj)	/ɪgˈzɔːstɪd/	erschöpft	**Exhausted** means 'very tired'.
exhibition (n)★★	/eksɪˈbɪʃən/	Ausstellung	They saw a great **exhibition** about the theatre in Shakespeare's time.
fact (n)★★★	/fækt/	Tatsache; Fakt	At the top of the page are some interesting **facts** about London.
have fun	/hæv ˈfʌn/	Spaß haben	Did you **have fun** this morning?
guys (form of address) (n pl)★★	/gaɪz/	Leute	Hi **guys**! Did you have fun this morning?
hurt (v)★★★	/hɜːt/	wehtun	Ow! My feet **hurt**!
ice cream (n)	/ˈaɪs kriːm/	Eis(krem)	Most people like eating **ice cream**.
later (adv)★★★	/ˈleɪtə/	spätter	He received the full payment 35 years **later**!
lazy (adj)★	/ˈleɪzi/	faul	Was Carol too **lazy** to climb the Monument?
lunch (n)★★★	/lʌntʃ/	Mittagessen	Let's have a picnic **lunch**!

Ow! (interj)	/aʊ/	Aua!	**Ow!** My feet hurt!
payment (n)★★★	/ˈpeɪmənt/	Bezahlung	He only received the second half of the **payment** 35 years later!
performance (n)★★★	/pəˈfɔːməns/	Vorstellung	The first **performance** at the new Globe was on 21st August, 1996.
picnic lunch (n)	/ˈpɪknɪk lʌntʃ/	Picknick zu Mittag	They have a **picnic lunch** in the park.
present (adj)★★★	/ˈprezənt/	jetzig	The **present** cathedral was designed by Sir Christopher Wren.
receive (v)★★★	/rɪˈsiːv/	erhalten	Wren didn't **receive** the second half of the payment for his work until the cathedral was complete.
record shop (n)	/ˈrekɔːd ʃɒp/	Schallplattengeschäft	I bought some CDs at a **record shop**.
spend (time) (v)★★★	/spend (ˈtaɪm)/	verbringen	We **spent** an hour at St Paul's.
stand (v)★★★	/stænd/	stehen	The Monument to the Great Fire **stands** near London Bridge.
step (n)★★★	/step/	Stufe	You must climb 311 **steps** to reach the top!
surf the Internet	/sɜːf ðiː ˈɪntənet/	im Internet surfen	Do you enjoy **surfing the Internet**?
thatched roof (n)	/ˈθætʃt ˈruːf/	Reetdach	The Globe Theatre is the first building in London with a **thatched roof** since the Great Fire!
the top (of) (n)★★★	/ðə ˈtɒp (əv)/	oben	There is a spectacular view from **the top** of the monument.
thirsty (adj)★	/ˈθɜːsti/	durstig	I'm **thirsty** – I need a drink!
tired (adj)★★★	/ˈtaɪəd/	müde	We climbed 311 steps and now we're very **tired**.
not ... until (prep)★★★	/ənˈtɪl/	erst	He didn't receive the second half of the payment **until** 1710.
work (n)★★★	/wɜːk/	Arbeit	Building **work** started in 1675.

3 What was he doing? (pp. 36–7)

at first	/ət ˈfɜːst/	zunächst	**At first** the sun was shining.
bicycle (n)	/ˈbaɪsɪkəl/	Fahrrad	Can you ride a **bicycle**?
big wheel (n)	/bɪg ˈwiːl/	Riesenrad	The London Eye is the slowest **big wheel** in the world.
bus (n)★★★	/bʌs/	Bus	Lots of people were waiting for the **bus**.
car (n)★★★	/kɑː/	Auto	Can you drive a **car**?
cruise (n)	/kruːz/	Bootsfahrt	The group go for a **cruise** on the River Thames.
cry (v)★★★	/kraɪ/	weinen	"Was Ben **crying**?" "No, he was laughing."
emergency number (n)	/ɪˈmɜːdʒənsi ˌnʌmbə/	Notdienst	He called the **emergency number** on his mobile phone.
fall (v)★★★	/fɔːl/	fallen	Ben **fell** into the river!
feel (v)★★★	/fiːl/	sich fühlen	Ben was **feeling** all right.
funny (adj)★★★	/ˈfʌni/	komisch	Laura took a photo of Ben because he looked **funny**!
helicopter (n)	/ˈhelɪkɒptə/	Hubschrauber	A police **helicopter** was flying in the sky.

hit (v)★★★	/hɪt/	gegen …..fahren	The boat **hit** a rock.
I've no idea.	/aɪv, nəʊ aɪˈdɪə/	Ich habe keine Ahnung.	"What was he doing?" "**I've no idea**."
laugh (v)★★★	/lɑːf/	lachen	He was shivering but he was **laughing**.
lifebelt (n)	/ˈlaɪfbelt/	Rettungsring	Greg threw Ben a **lifebelt** and pulled him out of the water.
overboard (adv)	/əʊvəˈbɔːd/	über Bord	Suddenly Ben fell **overboard** into the river.
pass (v)★★★	/pɑːs/	an ….vorbeigehen	We were **passing** the London Eye and suddenly Ben fell into the river!
plane (n)★★★	/pleɪn/	Flugzeug	It takes 7 hours from London to New York by **plane**.
point (v)★★★	/pɔɪnt/	auf etwas zeigen	Greg **pointed** at the London Eye.
pull (v)★★★	/pʊl/	ziehen	He **pulled** Ben out of the river.
rain (v)★	/reɪn/	regnen	"Was it **raining**?" "No, the sun was shining."
rescue (v)★	/ˈreskjuː/	retten	Ben tried to **rescue** his cap and fell into the river.
rock (n)★★★	/rɒk/	Fels	The boat hit a **rock** in a storm.
rocket (n)	/ˈrɒkɪt/	Rakete	When did the first **rocket** land on the moon?
sail (v)★★	/seɪl/	segeln	Lee was **sailing** with a friend off the coast of Africa.
shine (v)★	/ʃaɪn/	scheinen	The sun was **shining**.
shiver (v)	/ˈʃɪvə/	zittern	He was **shivering** with cold.
smile (v)★★★	/smaɪl/	lächeln	Tomek and Gabi **smiled** at Laura.
spaceship (n)	/ˈspeɪsʃɪp/	Raumschiff	A **spaceship** is a form of air transport.
speedboat (n)	/ˈspiːdbəʊt/	Schnellboot	A **speedboat** rescued them.
storm (n)★★	/stɔːm/	Sturm	**Storms** are dangerous when you are sailing.
suddenly (adv)★★★	/ˈsʌdənli/	plötzlich	**Suddenly** he fell into the river!
take a picture (of)	/teɪk ə ˈpɪktʃə (əv)/	ein Foto machen	Let me **take a picture** of you. Say 'cheese'!
terrific (adj)	/təˈrɪfɪk/	sagenhaft; klasse	The London Eye looks **terrific**! I'd love to go for a ride.
Thank goodness! (interj)	/θæŋk ˈɡʊdnəs/	Gott sei Dank!	"Greg pulled him out of the water!" "**Thank goodness!**"
whale (n)	/weɪl/	Wal	**Whales** are large mammals that live in the sea.
What on earth …?	/wɒt ɒn ˈɜːθ/	Was in Gottes Namen…; … bloß …?	**What on earth** was he doing?
whistle (v)	/ˈwɪsəl/	pfeifen	He walked past **whistling** happily.

4 Integrated Skills: Biography (pp. 38–9)

acting company (n)	/ˈæktɪŋ ˌkʌmpəni/	Schauspielgesellschaft	He joined an **acting company** and was soon writing plays.
beautiful (adj)★★★	/ˈbjuːtɪfəl/	schön	He wrote many **beautiful** poems.
bestseller (n)	/bestˈselə/	Bestseller	His books are still **bestsellers**.

Word	Pronunciation	German	Example
career (n)★★	/kəˈrɪə/	Laufbahn	In his early **career** he joined an acting company.
coast (n)★★	/kəʊst/	Küste	Portsmouth is on the south **coast** of England.
collect (v)★★★	/kəˈlekt/	sammeln	Two actor friends **collected** all his plays and published them.
death (n)★★★	/deθ/	Tod	After his **death** two actor friends published his plays.
decide (v)★★★	/dɪˈsaɪd/	beschließen	"When did he **decide** to leave Stratford." "In the late 1580s."
extremely (adv)★★★	/ɪkˈstriːmli/	äußerst; höchst	His plays were **extremely** popular.
factory (n)★★★	/ˈfæktri/	Fabrik	After he left school he started working in a **factory**.
fame (n)	/feɪm/	Ruhm	His **fame** as a playwright continues until the present day.
finally (adv)★★★	/ˈfaɪnəli/	zum Schluss	**Finally** he returned to Stratford in 1611.
fortune (n)★	/ˈfɔːtʃuːn/	Glück/Vermögen	If someone makes their **fortune** by doing something, they make a lot of money.
ghost story (n)	/ˈgəʊst stɔːri/	Gespenstergeschichte	A Christmas Carol is a **ghost story**.
join (v)★★★	/dʒɔɪn/	sich anschließen	Shakespeare **joined** an acting company in London.
major (adj)★★★	/ˈmeɪdʒə/	von größter Bedeutung	Oliver Twist and David Copperfield were two of Dickens's **major** novels.
move (to) (v)★★★	/muːv (tə)/	umziehen nach	His family **moved** to London when he was a boy.
newspaper (n)★★★	/ˈnjuːspeɪpə/	Zeitung	He started writing stories for **newspapers**.
next (adj)★★★	/nekst/	nächster, -e, -es	His success continued into the **next** century.
novel (n)★	/ˈnɒvəl/	Roman	His first **novel** was called The Pickwick Papers.
novelist (n)	/ˈnɒvəlɪst/	Romancier	A **novelist** writes novels.
part-owner (n)	/ˌpɑːt ˈəʊnə/	Teilinhaber	He became a rich man and **part-owner** of the Globe Theatre.
play (n)★★★	/pleɪ/	Theaterstück	Shakespeare wrote 37 **plays** in all.
playwright (n)	/ˈpleɪraɪt/	Dramatiker	He was a famous **playwright**.
probably (adv)★★★	/ˈprɒbəbli/	wahrscheinlich	He **probably** became a teacher.
publish (v)★★★	/ˈpʌblɪʃ/	veröffentlichen	Two actor friends **published** his plays in 1623.
rich (adj)★★★	/rɪtʃ/	reich	He became a **rich** man.
school (n)★★★	/skuːl/	Schule	"Where did he go to **school**?" "In Stratford."
several (adj)★★★	/ˈsevrəl/	mehrere	There were **several** theatres in London in the late 1580s.
soon (adv)★★★	/suːn/	bald	He joined an acting company and was **soon** writing plays.
story (n)★★★	/ˈstɔːri/	Geschichte	He wrote **stories** for newspapers.
success (n)★★★	/səkˈses/	Erfolg	Shakespeare's **success** continued into the seventeenth century.
teacher (n)★★★	/ˈtiːtʃə/	Lehrer	He went to school in Stratford and probably became a **teacher**.
tragedy (n)	/ˈtrædʒədi/	Tragödie	Hamlet and Othello are two of Shakespeare's most famous **tragedies**.
until (prep)★★★	/ənˈtɪl/	bis	He lived in Stratford from 1611 **until** he died.

well-known (adj)	/wel nəʊn/	(sehr) bekannt; berühmt	Shakespeare soon became a **well-known** actor and playwright.
when (adv)★★★	/wen/	als	**When** he was 18 Shakespeare married Anne Hathaway.
work (v)★★★	/wɜːk/	arbeiten	He **worked** most of his life in London.
writer (n)★★★	/raɪtə/	Schriftsteller	He is one of the most famous **writers** in the world.

Inspiration *Extra!* (pp. 40–41)

cassette (n)	/kəˈset/	Kassette	You can buy Shakespeare's plays on **cassette**.
cassette recorder (n)	/kəˈset rɪˌkɔːdə/	Kassettenrecorder	You use a **cassette recorder** for listening to cassettes.
impossible (adj)★★★	/ɪmˈpɒsɪbəl/	unmöglich	"There's Shakespeare's computer." "No, that's **impossible!**"
record (v)★★★	/rɪˈkɔːd/	aufnehmen	You can **record** music and songs on a cassette recorder.
typewriter (n)	/ˈtaɪpraɪtə/	Schreibmaschine	Shakespeare used a **typewriter** not a computer!

Culture: Hello New York! (pp. 42–3)

apartment (n) (AmE)★	/əˈpɑːtmənt/	Wohnung	**Apartment** is the American English word for a 'flat'.
area (n)★★★	/ˈeəriə/	Fläche; Gebiet	A large **area** covered with trees is called a forest.
biscuit (n) (BrE)	/ˈbɪskɪt/	Keks	The American English word for **biscuit** is 'cookie'.
car park (n) (BrE)	/kɑː pɑːk/	Parkplatz	'Parking lot' is the American English word for **car park**.
cell phone (n) (AmE)	/ˈsel fəʊn/	Handy	**Cell phone** is the American English word for a 'mobile phone'.
chips (n pl) (BrE) ★★	/tʃɪps/	Pommes frites	In British English they say **chips**, in American English they say 'French fries'.
covered with★★★	/ˈkʌvəd wɪð/	voller	A forest is a large area **covered with** trees.
discover (v)★★★	/dɪsˈkʌvə/	entdecken	An Englishman **discovered** the Hudson River.
drugstore (n) (AmE)	/ˈdrʌgstɔː/	Apotheke(r)	**Drugstore** is the American English word for a 'chemist's'.
Dutch (adj)	/dʌtʃ/	holländisch; niederländisch	The original **Dutch** name for New York was New Amsterdam.
the Dutch (n)	/ðə dʌtʃ/	die Holländer	**The Dutch** came to live in New York in 1624.
explorer (n)	/ɪkˈsplɔːrə/	Forscher; Entdecker	Giovanni da Verrazano, an Italian **explorer**, discovered New York harbour in 1524.
flat (BrE) (n)★★	/flæt/	Wohnung	**Flat** is the British English word for an 'apartment'.
forest (n)★★★	/ˈfɒrɪst/	Forst; Wald	A **forest** is a large area that is covered with trees.
French fries (n pl) (AmE)	/ˌfrentʃ ˈfraɪz/	Pommes frites	In American English they say **French fries**, in British English they say 'chips'.
garbage (n) (AmE)	/ˈgɑːbɪdʒ/	Müll	**Garbage** is the American English word for 'rubbish'.
grammar (n)★★	/ˈgræmə/	Grammatik	The **grammar** of American English is very similar to British English.
harbour (n)	/ˈhɑːbə/	Hafen	An Italian explorer sailed into New York **harbour** in 1524.

island (n)★★★	/ˈaɪlənd/	Insel	The **island** that is today called Manhattan was originally called Mannahatta island.
Native American (n)	/ˌneɪtɪv əˈmerɪkən/	einheimische Amerikaner	Only a few hundred years ago, the only people to live in New York were **Native Americans**.
nonsense (n)★	/ˈnɒnsəns/	Unsinn	The word 'poppycock' is a word of Dutch origin meaning **nonsense**.
pants (n pl) (AmE)	/pænts/	Hose	**Pants** is the American English word for 'trousers'.
parking lot (n) (AmE)	/ˈpɑːkɪŋ lɒt/	Parkplatz	'Car park' is the British English word for **parking lot**.
piece (n)★★★	/piːs/	Stück	A **piece** of land with water around it is called an island.
railroad (n) (AmE)	/ˈreɪlrəʊd/	Eisenbahn	**Railroad** in American English means the same as 'railway'.
railway (n) (BrE)★★★	/ˈreɪlweɪ/	Eisenbahn	**Railway** in British English means the same as 'railroad'.
sneakers (n pl) (AmE)	/ˈsniːkəz/	Sportschuhe; Turnschuhe	The American English word **sneakers** means the same as the British English 'trainers'.
store (n) (AmE)★★	/stɔː/	Laden; Geschäft	A **store** means the same as a 'shop' in British English.
trash (n) (AmE)	/træʃ/	Müll	**Trash** is the American English word for 'rubbish'.
vocabulary (n)★	/vəʊˈkæbjʊləri/	Wortschatz	The **vocabulary** of British and American English is often different.

Unit 4

1 Is he going to shoot someone? (pp. 44–5)

act (v)★★★	/ækt/	Schauspieler sein/werden	Would you like to **act** as a career?
action (n)★★★	/ˈækʃən/	Achtung! Aufnahme!	Silence everyone! **Action**!
appear (v)★★★	/əˈpɪə/	teilnehmen; auftreten	Have you ever **appeared** on a TV quiz?
Best wishes (as formula for ending letter)	/best ˈwɪʃɪz/	Mit den besten Wünschen	Looking forward to hearing from you. **Best wishes**, Erik.
a bit (adv)★★★	/ə ˈbɪt/	ein bisschen	Move over **a bit** – I can't see.
boring (adj)★★	/ˈbɔːrɪŋ/	langweilig	Carol thinks soaps are really **boring**.
camp (v)	/kæmp/	zelten; campen	They're going to **camp** by the coast for their holidays.
camping site (n)	/ˈkæmpɪŋ saɪt/	Campingplatz	The **camping site** is open from April to October.
cast (n)	/kɑːst/	Besetzung; Mitwirkende	The **cast** is the group of actors in a TV programme, film or play.
chair (n)★★★	/tʃeə/	Stuhl	There's a **chair** in the picture just behind Kate.
cheap (adj)★★★	/tʃiːp/	billig	Erik and Carlos can get **cheap** tickets because they're students.

crazy (adj)★★	/'kreɪzi/	verrückt	You're **crazy**! Give me the gun!
curtains (n pl)★★★	/'kɜ:tən/	Vorhänge	Can you see the long blue **curtains** in the background?
drum (n)★	/drʌm/	Schlagzeug	He plays the **drums** in a band as a hobby.
the future (n)★★★	/ðə 'fju:tʃə/	Zukunft	Liam won't be in *Westsiders* in **the future**.
gun (n)★★★	/gʌn/	Schusswaffe; Kanone	You're crazy! Give me the **gun**!
kill (v)★★★	/kɪl/	töten	Is he going to **kill** someone with that gun?
microphone (n)	/'maɪkrəfəʊn/	Mikrofon	A **microphone** makes your voice sound louder.
move over (phr v)	/mu:v 'əʊvə/	zur Seite rücken	I can't see a thing – **move over** a bit.
plan (n)★★★	/plæn/	Plan	What are your **plans** for the holidays?
recording (n)	/rɪ'kɔ:dɪŋ/	Aufnahme	Would you like to act in a **recording** of *Westsiders*?
rehearsal (n)	/rɪ'hɜ:səl/	Probe	In a minute we're going to watch the *Westsiders* **rehearsal**.
rehearse (v)	/rɪ'hɜ:s/	proben	The actors are going to start **rehearsing** now.
shoot (v)★★★	/ʃu:t/	erschießen	Do you think that man's going to **shoot** someone with that gun?
silence (n)★★	/'saɪləns/	Ruhe	**Silence** everyone! Action!
soap (opera) (n)★★	/'səʊp ˌɒprə/	Seifenoper	*Westsiders* is a **soap** like *Neighbours* or *Friends*.
student (n)★★★	/'stju:dənt/	Student(in)	**Students** get cheap tickets.
studio (n)★★	/'stju:diəʊ/	Studio	The group are visiting the YTV **studio**.
surf (v)	/sɜ:f/	surfen	Several people were **surfing** on the waves.
surprise (n)★★★	/sə'praɪz/	Überraschung	"What kind of a treat is it?" "I'm not going to tell you – it's a **surprise**."
swim (v)★★	/swɪm/	schwimmen	Do you like **swimming** in the sea?
treat (n)	/tri:t/	besondere Freude	There's a special **treat** for you this afternoon. It's going to be a surprise.
well (adj)★	/wel/	wohlauf; (geht es … gut?)	"Are you **well**?" "Yes, we're fine."
worry (v)★★★	/'wʌri/	sich Sorgen machen	Don't **worry**, I'm not going to kill anyone.

2 I'll miss him (pp. 46–7)

afraid (adj)★★★	/ə'freɪd/	Angst haben	Are you **afraid** of dogs?
anyone (pron)★★★	/'eniwʌn/	jemand	"When Liam leaves the show I won't have **anyone** to talk to," said Peter.
have an argument	/hæv ən 'ɑ:gjəmənt/	sich streiten	We're not friends anymore – we've **had an argument**.
cartoon (n)	/kɑ:'tu:n/	Cartoon	I like watching **cartoons** on the Disney Channel.
cat (n)★★★	/kæt/	Katze	Do you prefer **cats** or dogs?
chat show (n)	/'tʃæt ˌʃəʊ/	Talkshow	**Chat shows** are programmes in which interviewers interview famous guests.
drama (n)★	/'drɑ:mə/	Drama	A **drama** is a play shown on TV in which exciting things happen.
documentary (n)	/dɒkjə'mentəri/	Dokumentarfilm	We watched a **documentary** about tigers in danger of extinction.

free (adj)★★★	/friː/	frei; entlassen	Simon went to prison but is now **free**.
game show (n)	/ɡeɪm ʃəʊ/	Gamesshow	**Games shows** are programmes in which people answer questions or do things in order to win a prize.
get on (well) (phr v)	/ɡet 'ɒn/	sich gut verstehen	"We **get on** really well together and I loved working with him," said Emma.
have a go	/hæv ə 'ɡəʊ/	einen Versuch wagen	Jack will probably let everyone else **have a go** first – he's not interested in computer games.
keep in touch	/ˌkiːp ɪn 'tʌtʃ/	in Kontakt bleiben	We'll miss you. Please **keep in touch**.
manager (n)★★	/mænɪdʒə/	Manager	Robbie is the **manager** of Blacks, a pool club.
music programme (n)	/mjuːzɪk ˌprəʊɡræm/	Musiksendung	It's a weekly **music programme** in which bands and artists sing their latest songs.
news programme (n)	/njuːz ˌprəʊɡræm/	Nachrichtensendung	The **news programme** is on at 7 o'clock every evening.
pool (n)★★	/puːl/	Pool(billard)	**Pool** is a game similar to snooker or billiards.
pleased (adj)★★	/pliːzd/	erfreut	Carol won't be **pleased** because she doesn't like soaps.
prefer (v)★★★	/prɪ'fɜː/	bevorzugen; lieber haben	Which do you **prefer** – cats or dogs?
prison (n)★★★	/prɪzn/	Gefängnis	People who commit crimes go to **prison**.
relationship (n)★★★	/rɪ'leɪʃənʃɪp/	Beziehung	Peter and Liam had a really good **relationship**.
revenge (n)	/rɪ'vendʒ/	Rache	Simon wants **revenge** on Robbie because he went to prison for something Robbie had done.
rope (n)★★	/rəʊp/	Seil; Strick	Do you think Simon will tie Robbie up with the **rope**?
sports programme (n)	/spɔːts ˌprəʊɡræm/	Sportsendung	We watched highlights of the match on the **sports programme**.
terribly (adv)	/terɪbli/	furchtbar	Emma will miss Liam **terribly**.
theft (n)	/θeft/	Diebstahl	He went to prison for **theft** after stealing £10,000 from a bank.
thriller (n)	/θrɪlə/	Thriller	A **thriller** is an exciting and frightening film, often about a crime.
tie up (phr v)	/taɪ 'ʌp/	festbinden	Will Simon **tie** Robbie **up** with the rope?
valuable (adj)★★	/væljʊbəl/	wertvoll; kostbar	Something that is **valuable** is worth a lot of money.
walk (n)★★	/wɔːk/	Spaziergang	I must take the dog for a **walk**.

3 You spoke too fast (pp. 48–9)

absurd (adj)	/əb'sɜːd/	absurd	"The director thinks you spoke too fast." "That's **absurd**! We just spoke normally."
activity (n)★★★	/æk'tɪvɪti/	Aktivität	Drama exercises are practice **activities** for actors.
I'm afraid (= I'm sorry)	/aɪm ə'freɪd/	Tut mir Leid …	**I'm afraid** the director thinks you acted badly.

angrily (adv)	/ˈæŋɡrɪli/	verärgert	"That's absurd!" she said **angrily**.
badly (adv)★★	/ˈbædli/	schlecht	The director thinks the group acted **badly**.
bossily (adv)	/ˈbɒsɪli/	herrisch	"Put it there!" she said **bossily**.
broadcast (n)	/ˈbrɔːdkɑːst/	Sendung; Übertragung	A **broadcast** is a show on television.
broadcast (v)	/ˈbrɔːdkɑːst/	senden; übertragen	YTV aren't going to **broadcast** the *Westsiders* episode you recorded.
character (n)★★★	/ˈkærɪktə/	Rolle; Figur	Liam Swan plays the **character** Robbie.
comfortable (adj)★★	/ˈkʌmftəbəl/	bequem	You don't look very **comfortable** sitting on the edge of the chair!
comfortably (adv)	/ˈkʌmftəbli/	bequem	Is everyone sitting **comfortably**?
drama exercise (n)	/ˈdrɑːmə(r) ˈeksəsaɪz/	Schauspielübung	**Drama exercises** help actors become better at their job.
early (adv)★★★	/ˈɜːli/	früh(zeitig)	Try to arrive **early**.
episode (n)	/ˈepɪsəʊd/	Folge; Episode	Watch the next **episode** and find out what happens.
fast (adv)★★★	/fɑːst/	schnell	I'm afraid the director thinks you spoke too **fast**.
happily (adv)	/ˈhæpɪli/	glücklich	"Hello," he said, smiling **happily**.
hard (adv)★★★	/hɑːd/	hart	Actors work really **hard** and spend hours doing drama exercises.
late (adv)★★★	/leɪt/	spat	Why do buses always arrive **late**?
loudly (adv)	/ˈlaʊdli/	laut	**Loudly** is the opposite of 'quietly'.
need (v)★★★	/niːd/	brauchen	Jack thinks they **needed** a longer rehearsal.
nervous (adj)★★	/ˈnɜːvəs/	nervös	It's normal to feel **nervous** before an exam.
nervously (adv)	/ˈnɜːvəsli/	nervös	"Sorry I'm late," she said **nervously**.
(bad) news (n)★★★	/ˈ(bæd) njuːz/	schlechte Nachricht	I'm afraid I've got some bad **news** for you.
normally (adv)★★★	/ˈnɔːməli/	normal	We just spoke **normally**, that's all.
ourselves (pron)★★	/aʊˈselvz/	selbst	But we weren't acting. We were being **ourselves**.
performance (n)★★★	/pəˈfɔːməns/	Vorstellung	The next **performance** starts at 20.30.
politely (adv)	/pəˈlaɪtli/	höflich	"May I have a biscuit?" he asked **politely**.
practise (v)★★	/ˈpræktɪs/	üben	If you rehearse a play, TV programme etc, you **practise** it.
properly (adv)★★	/ˈprɒpəli/	richtig; ordentlich	We didn't have enough time to rehearse **properly**.
quickly (adv)★★★	/ˈkwɪkli/	schnell	The director thinks they spoke too **quickly**.
quietly (adv)★★★	/ˈkwaɪətli/	ruhig	**Quietly** is the opposite of 'loudly'.
rudely (adv)	/ˈruːdli/	unhöflich; unsanft	She pushed past them **rudely** without saying "Excuse me."
sad (adj)★★	/sæd/	traurig	In the photo Laura and Tomek look very **sad**.
sadly (adv)	/ˈsædli/	traurig	"I'm sorry," said Kate, smiling **sadly**.
What a shame!	/wɒt ə ˈʃeɪm/	Wie schade!	"They're not going to broadcast the episode you recorded." **"What a shame!** Why not?"

slowly (adv)★★★	/ˈsləʊli/	langsam	Could you speak a bit more **slowly**, please?
well (adv)★★★	/wel/	gut	Kate thinks the group did **well** but the director thinks they acted badly.

4 Integrated Skills: TV programmes (pp. 50–51)

accident (n)★★★	/ˈæksɪdənt/	Unfall	He was killed in a terrible car **accident**.
action-packed (adj)	/ˈækʃən pækt/	voller Action	Episodes of *Casualty* are **action-packed**, with accidents, serious illnesses and emergencies.
adjective (n)★	/ˈædʒektɪv/	Adjektiv	An **adjective** is a word, such as 'interesting' or 'long' that describes another word.
adverb (n)★	/ˈædvɜːb/	Adverb	'Badly', 'fast' and 'slowly' are all examples of **adverbs**.
backwards (adv)★	/ˈbækwədz/	rückwärts	One episode was about the life of a dying woman who decided to do everything **backwards**!
caravan park (n)	/ˈkærəvæn pɑːk/	Parkplatz für Wohnwagen	A **caravan park** is a place where people live in caravans.
carefully (adv)	/ˈkeəfəli/	vorsichtig; wohlüberlegt	Think **carefully** before you answer.
copy (v)★★★	/ˈkɒpi/	nachahmen	Some people try to **copy** the lives of soap stars in real life.
doctor (n)★★★	/ˈdɒktə/	Arzt	*Casualty* is about the lives and loves of **doctors** and nurses.
easily (adv)★★★	/ˈiːzɪli/	leicht	I answered all the questions **easily**.
emergency (n)★★	/ɪˈmɜːdʒənsi/	Notfall	An **emergency** is a serious situation that you must deal with immediately.
fast-moving (adj)	/ˈfɑːst muːvɪŋ/	mit schnellen Handlungsabläufen	A good soap should be **fast-moving** and have plenty of exciting action.
gerund (n)	/ˈdʒerənd/	Gerundium	A **gerund** is a noun formed from a verbs such as the word 'waiting' in the sentence: "I can't stand waiting for people".
hospital (n)★★★	/ˈhɒspɪtəl/	Krankenhaus	*Casualty* is about the doctors, nurses and patients in a **hospital**.
hungrily (adv)	/ˈhʌŋɡrɪli/	hungrig	She ate her sandwich **hungrily**.
illness (n)★★★	/ˈɪlnəs/	Krankheit	A lot of the patients in *Casualty* are suffering from serious **illnesses**.
imaginary (adj)	/ɪˈmædʒɪnri/	fiktiv; erfunden	Ramsay Street is the **imaginary** place where *Neighbours* takes place.
infinitive (n)	/ɪnˈfɪnɪtɪv/	Infinitiv	Use "going to" + **infinitive** to talk about future plans.
local (adj)★	/ˈləʊkəl/	Stammlokal	The **local** pub in *EastEnders* is called the Queen Vic.
murderer (n)	/ˈmɜːdərə/	Mörder(in)	A **murderer** is someone who deliberately kills someone else.
noun (n)★	/naʊn/	Substantiv	Add 's to a singular **noun** to form the possessive, for example "the producer's job", "Gabi's T-shirt".
nurse (n)	/nɜːs/	Krankenschwester	Hospital soaps are about the lives and loves of doctors and **nurses**.

patient (n)	/ˈpeɪʃnt/	Patient	Lots of people love following the lives of doctors, nurses and their **patients** in *Casualty*.
performer (n)	/pəˈfɔːmə/	Künstler(in); Schauspieler(in)	The most famous **performer** in *Neighbours* is Kylie Minogue.
preposition (n)	/prepəˈzɪʃən/	Präposition	"Behind", "in front of" and "opposite" are all examples of **prepositions**.
pronoun (n)	/ˈprəʊnaʊn/	Pronomen	"Mine,"yours", "his" and "hers" are all examples of possessive **pronouns**.
pub (n)★★	/pʌb/	Kneipe; Lokal	The Queen Vic is the name of the local **pub** in *EastEnders*.
recent (adj)★★★	/ˈriːsənt/	neuester, -e, -es	In a **recent** episode there was a terrible train crash.
robbery (n)	/ˈrɒbəri/	Raub(überfall); Einbruch	A **robbery** is a situation in which criminals go into a house or other building and steal things.
romance (n)	/rəʊˈmæns/	Liebesgeschichte	A good soap should have action as well as **romance**.
serious (adj)★★★	/ˈsɪəriəs/	schwer; ernsthaft	Many of the patients are suffering from **serious** illnesses.
setting (n)★	/ˈsetɪŋ/	Schauplatz	Summer Bay is the imaginary **setting** for the Australian soap *Home and Away*.
singer (n)	/ˈsɪŋə/	Sänger(in)	Kylie Minogue became a famous **singer**.
take place	/teɪk ˈpleɪs/	stattfinden	"Where does the action of *Home and Away* **take place**?" "In Summer Bay.
thirstily (adv)	/ˈθɜːstɪli/	durstig	It was very hot outside and they drank the water **thirstily**.
trouble (n)★★★	/ˈtrʌbəl/	Ärger	There's always **trouble** in soap operas – arguments, fights, robberies.
understand (v)★★★	/ʌndəˈstænd/	verstehen	If you speak too quickly they won't **understand** you.
verb (n)★	/vɜːb/	Verb; zeitwort	A **verb** is a word that describes an action such as "go", "do" or "walk".
village (n)★★★	/ˈvɪlɪdʒ/	Dorf	*Emmerdale* is about life in a **village** in Yorkshire, England.

Review Units 1–2 (pp. 54–5)

accept★★★	/əkˈsept/	annehmen	She nearly didn't **accept** the part because there's a lot of singing in the film.
beautifully (adv)	/ˈbjuːtɪfli/	schön; prima	Everything is working out well, **beautifully**, in fact.
busy (adj)★★★	/ˈbɪzi/	beschäftigt	Nick thinks Tamsin will be too **busy** to think of him.
close (v)★★★	/kləʊz/	schließen	**Close** your eyes – I've got a surprise for you.
explain (v)★★★	/ɪkˈspleɪn/	erklären	"I nearly didn't accept the part because there's a lot of singing," Tamsin **explained**.
film (v)	/fɪlm/	verfilmen	Tamsin has now finished **filming** *Westsiders*.
promise (v)★★★	/ˈprɒmɪs/	versprechen	I **promise** I'll come and join you as soon as I can.
ready (adj)★★★	/ˈredi/	fertig; sich vorbereiten	"What are you doing now?" "I'm getting **ready** for the trip to California."
time difference (n)	/taɪm dɪfrəns/	Zeitunterschied	There's an 8-hour **time difference** between California and London.

trip (n)★★	/trɪp/	Reise	She's really looking forward to the **trip** to California.
work out (phr v)	/wɜːk ˈaʊt/	klappen; gelingen	"Everything is **working out** beautifully," she said.
worried (adj)★	/ˈwʌrɪd/	besorgt	I'm a bit **worried** about pickpockets.

Unit 5

1 What's happening tomorrow? (pp. 56–7)

arrangement (n)★★★	/əˈreɪndʒmənt/	Vorbereitungen	The diary on p. 56 shows the **arrangements** for Saturday.
commercial (n)	/kəˈmɜːʃəl/	Werbespot	The group are going to watch the filming of a jeans **commercial**.
perfect (adj)★★	/ˈpɜːfɪkt/	perfekt	We really enjoyed the holiday – in fact, it was **perfect**.
underground (n)	/ˈʌndəɡraʊnd/	U-bahn	To get to the Science Museum, take the **underground** to South Kensington.

2 You can't miss it! (pp. 58–9)

across (prep)★★★	/əˈkrɒs/	(quer) über	Go **across** Park Lane.
along (prep)★★★	/əˈlɒŋ/	entlang	You go straight **along** Oxford Street past a store called Selfridges.
Come on!★★★	/kʌm ˈɒn/	Komm; Los	**Come on**, Carol, let's run!
corner (n)★★★	/ˈkɔːnə/	Ecke	I'm sure the shop is just round the **corner**.
department store (n)	/dɪˈpɑːtmənt stɔː/	Kaufhaus	A **department store** is a very large shop that sells a lot of different things.
far (adj)★★★	/fɑː/	weit	Don't worry. James Street isn't very **far**.
Hurry up!★	/ˈhʌri ˈʌp/	Beeilung!; Mach schnell!	**Hurry up**, Ben! I'm waiting for you!
into (prep)★★★	/ˈɪntuː ˈɪntə,/	in	Turn right **into** Oxford Street.
left (adv)	/left/	links	Turn **left** into James Street.
the left (n)★★	/ðə left/	links; auf der linken Seite	James Street is the third street on **the left**.
miss (= not see) (v)★★★	/mɪs/	verpassen; übersehen	Turn left into James Street and Teen Jeans is on the right. You can't **miss** it.
past (prep)★★★	/pɑːst/	an … vorbei	Go along Oxford Street **past** a department store called Selfridges.
police officer (n)	/pəˈliːs ɒfɪsə/	Polizist; Polizeibeamter(in)	Look, there's a **police officer** – I'll ask her the way.
right (adv)★★★	/raɪt/	rechts	Walk up to Oxford Street and turn **right**.
the right (n)★★★	/ðə raɪt/	rechts; auf der rechten Seite	Teen Jeans is on **the right**.
round (prep)★★★	/raʊnd/	um	The shop is just **round** the corner – I'm sure.

through (prep)★★★	/θruː/	durch	Walk **through** Hyde Park to Marble Arch.
to (prep)★★★	/tuː, tə/	bis	Walk through Hyde Park **to** Marble Arch.
turn left/right	/tɜːn 'left 'raɪt/	links abbiegen	**Turn left** into James Street.
up (prep)★★★	/ʌp/	hinauf	Go **up** this street to Oxford Street and turn right.

3 Could I borrow some money? (pp. 60–61)

borrow (v)★★	/ˈbɒrəʊ/	borgen; sich leihen	I haven't got any money. Could I **borrow** some?
bread (n)★★★	/bred/	Brot	Can we also order garlic **bread**?
certainly (adv)★★★	/ˈsɜːtənli/	gewiss; sicher	"Can I have a glass of water?" "**Certainly**."
cheese (n)★★	/tʃiːz/	Käse	I'll have **cheese** instead of a dessert.
customer (n)★★★	/ˈkʌstəmə/	Kunde(in)	A waiter's job is to serve **customers** in a restaurant or café.
dairy produce (n)	/ˈdeəri ˈprɒdjuːs/	Milchprodukte	Cheese, eggs and milk are all types of **dairy produce**.
extra (adj)★★★	/ˈekstrə/	extra	Could I have **extra** cheese on my pizza?
fried egg (n)	/fraɪd 'eg/	Spiegelei	Bacon and **fried eggs** is the traditional English breakfast.
garlic (n)	/ˈgɑːlɪk/	Knoblauch	Don't eat too much **garlic** or your breath will smell!
garlic bread (n)	/ˈgɑːlɪk bred/	Knoblauchbrot	Can we order some **garlic bread** too, please?
glass (n)★★★	/glɑːs/	Glas	Just a **glass** of water for me, please.
ham (n)	/hæm/	Schinken	"Try the Four Seasons Pizza." "I'm a vegetarian and I don't like **ham**."
honestly (adv)	/ˈɒnəstli/	ehrlich	**Honestly**, you're hopeless!
hopeless (adj)	/ˈhəʊpləs/	hoffnungslos	Honestly, Ben, you're **hopeless**!
meat (n)★★★	/miːt/	Fleisch	Ham is the pink **meat** that comes from a pig.
mushroom (n)	/ˈmʌʃrʊm/	Pilz	If you like **mushrooms**, try the Four Seasons Pizza.
olive (n)	/ˈɒlɪv/	Olive	Do you prefer green or black **olives**?
onion (n)	/ˈʌnjən/	Zwiebel	**Onions** are used a lot in cooking to add flavour to food.
order (v)★★★	/ˈɔːdə/	bestellen	The waiter asked them if they were ready to **order**.
pepper (n)	/ˈpepə/	Paprika	The Country Pizza has a topping of cheese, onions, mushrooms and green and red **peppers**.
pineapple (n)	/ˈpaɪnæpəl/	Ananas	A **pineapple** is a large fruit with yellow flesh.
spinach (n)	/ˈspɪnɪdʒ/	Spinat	**Spinach** is a green vegetable that a lot of people don't like, but it's good for you.
starving (I'm ...) (adj)	/ˈstɑːvɪŋ/	Ich sterbe vor Hunger.	Let's choose something to eat. I'm **starving**!
table (n)★★★	/ˈteɪbəl/	Tisch	There are no glasses on the **table**.
tomato (n)	/təˈmɑːtəʊ/	Tomate	The Country Pizza and the Tropical Pizza don't have **tomatoes**.
vegetarian (adj)	/vedʒəˈteəriən/	vegetarisch; Vegetarier	If you're **vegetarian**, try our Country Pizza.

4 Integrated Skills: Suggestions and advice (pp. 62–3)

abbreviation (abbrev) (n)	/əbriːvɪ'eɪʃən/	Abkürzung	EU is an **abbreviation** for European Union.
absorb (v)	/əb'zɔːb/	absorbieren	Cotton **absorbs** water and takes a long time to dry.
advice (n)★★★	/əd'vaɪs/	Ratschläge	The article on p. 62 contains **advice** for backpackers.
alternative (n)★★	/ɔːl'tɜːnətɪv/	Alternative	The modern **alternative** to a wool sweater is a fleece.
annoying (adj)★	/ə'nɔɪɪŋ/	lasting; ärgerlich	It can be very **annoying** wearing a backpack on a crowded bus or train.
artificial (adj)★	/ɑːtɪ'fɪʃəl/	künstlich; Kunst-	Polyester is cloth made from **artificial** material.
auxiliary verb (aux)	/ɔːk'zɪliəri ˌvɜːb/	Hilfsverb	In the sentence "I am leaving", 'am' is an **auxiliary verb**.
backpack (n)	/'bækpæk/	Rucksack	A **backpack** is a large bag for carrying things in that you wear on your back.
backpacker (n)	/'bækpækə/	Backpacker	The article on p. 62 is full of suggestions and advice for **backpackers**.
backpacking (n)	/'bækpækɪŋ/	auf Wandertour	I went **backpacking** round Australia last summer.
cardboard box (n)	/kɑːdbɔːd 'bɒks/	Pappschachtel	First put all the things you want to take in a **cardboard box**, then choose only a third of them!
cheaply (adv)	/'tʃiːpli/	billig	Backpackers are tourists who travel **cheaply**.
cloth (n)★★★	/klɒθ/	Stoff	Cotton is a type of **cloth**.
cotton (n)★★	/'kɒtən/	Baumwolle	Don't wear **cotton** next to your skin – it takes a long time to dry.
countable (C)	/'kaʊntəbəl/	zählbar	**Countable** nouns have a singular and a plural form.
crowded (adj)★	/'kraʊdɪd/	überfüllt; voll besetzt	It's uncomfortable standing on a **crowded** bus or train wearing a backpack.
daypack (n)	/'deɪpæk/	Tasche mit dem Tagesbedarf	A **daypack** is a smaller bag for carrying things like bottles of water when you're sightseeing.
dry (v)★★	/draɪ/	trocknen	Cotton absorbs water and takes a long time to **dry**.
experienced (adj)★	/ɪk'spɪərɪənst/	erfahren	**Experienced** travellers suggest you should not take too many things with you.
heavy (adj)★★★	/'hevi/	schwer	An ordinary raincoat is no good when it rains because it's too **heavy**.
instead (adv)★★★	/ɪn'sted/	stattdessen	Don't take cotton T-shirts. Get polyester ones **instead**.
keep warm	/kiːp 'wɔːm/	warm bleiben	Wearing a fleece is a good way to **keep warm**.
lightweight (adj)	/'laɪtweɪt/	leicht	A **lightweight** waterproof jacket is a better idea than a raincoat.
material (n)★★★	/mə'tɪərɪəl/	Material	"What sort of **material** is your T-shirt made of?" "Polyester."
ordinary (adj)★★★	/'ɔːdənri/	normal; gewöhnlich	An **ordinary** raincoat is no good when it rains.

plural (pl) (adj)★	/ˈpluərəl/	Mehrzahl; Plural	"Children" is a **plural** noun.
polyester (n)	/ˌpɒliˈestə/	Polyester	**Polyester** dries more quickly than cotton.
raincoat (n)	/ˈreɪnkəʊt/	Regenmantel	When it rains an ordinary **raincoat** is no good because it's too heavy.
realise (v)★★★	/ˈrɪəlaɪz/	verstehen	Most people **realise** that carrying things in a suitcase is a bad idea if you're going round the world.
rucksack (n)	/ˈrʌksæk/	Rucksack	A travel sack has straps so you can wear it on your shoulders like a **rucksack**.
shoulder (n)★★★	/ˈʃəʊldə/	Schulter	The things on a rucksack which go over your **shoulders** are called 'straps'.
singular (sing) (adj)	/ˈsɪŋgjələ/	Einzahl; Singular	'Man' is the **singular** form and 'men' is the plural form.
skin (n)★★★	/skɪn/	Haut	Don't wear cotton next to your **skin** – it takes a long time to dry.
somebody (sb)★★★	/ˈsʌmbədi/	jemand	'Sb' is the abbreviation for **somebody**.
something (sth)★★★	/ˈsʌmθɪŋ/	etwas	'Sth' is the abbreviation for **something**.
strap (n)	/stræp/	Gurt; Riemen	**Straps** are the things on a rucksack or backpack that go over your shoulders.
strong (adj)★★★	/strɒŋ/	kräftig	Jeans are **strong** but take a long time to dry.
stuff (n)★★★	/stʌf/	Zeug	How much **stuff** can you take in a travel sack?
suggest (v)★★★	/səˈdʒest/	vorschlagen; empfehlen	Experienced travellers **suggest** you should not take too much stuff with you.
suggestion (n)★★★	/səˈdʒestʃən/	Vorschlag	Can I make a **suggestion**?
suit (n)★★	/suːt/	Anzug	My father always wears a **suit** to work.
suitcase (n)	/ˈsuːtkeɪs/	Koffer	You carry a **suitcase** in your hands but you can't wear it on your back!
sweater (n)	/ˈswetə/	Sweater; Pullover	The modern alternative to a wool **sweater** is a fleece.
swimming trunks (n pl)	/ˈswɪmɪŋ trʌŋks/	Badehose	**Swimming trunks** are the things men and boys wear to swim in.
a third (n)	/ə ˈθɜːd/	ein Drittel	Put all the things you want to take in a cardboard box, then choose only **a third** of them!
tie (n)★	/taɪ/	Krawatte	He wanted to look smart so decided to wear a shirt and **tie**.
tip (= suggestion) (n)★	/tɪp/	Tipp	There are lots of good **tips** for backpackers in the article on p. 62.
travel sack (n)	/ˈtrævəl sæk/	große Reisetasche	A **travel sack** is a big bag which you can carry like a suitcase or wear on your back like a rucksack.
travel writer (n)	/ˈtrævəl ˌraɪtə/	Verfasser von Reiseberichten	**Travel writer** Hilary Bradt doesn't think a rucksack or a suitcase is a good idea when you're travelling.
traveller (n)★	/ˈtrævlə/	Reisende(r)	They're experienced **travellers** who have been all over the world.
turn round (phr v)★★★	/tɜːn ˈraʊnd/	sich umdrehen	It's difficult to **turn round** if you wear a backpack on a crowded bus or train.

uncountable (U) (adj)	/ʌnˈkaʊntəbəl/	unzählbar	'Rice', 'spaghetti' and 'milk' are all **uncountable** nouns – you can't use 'a' or 'an' with them.
wash (v)★★★	/wɒʃ/	waschen	Polyester-cotton trousers are easy to **wash** and dry.
waterproof (adj)	/ˈwɔːtəpruːf/	wasserdicht	**Waterproof** clothes stop you from getting wet.
wool (n)★★	/wʊl/	Wolle	The modern alternative to a **wool** sweater is a fleece.

Inspiration *Extra!* (pp. 64–5)

closed (adj)★★	/kləʊzd/	geschlossen	Sorry, the restaurant is **closed** now.
down (prep)★★★	/daʊn/	hinunter	Turn left outside Teen Jeans and walk **down** to Oxford Street.
fork (n)★	/fɔːk/	Gabel	A **fork** is a thing with three or four sharp points used for eating food.
huge (adj)★★★	/hjuːdʒ/	riesig	**Huge** means 'very large'.
knife (n)★★★	/naɪf/	Messer	A **knife** is a thing you use for cutting food when you are eating.
madam (form of address) (n)	/ˈmædəm/	gnädige Frau	"A table for two, please." "Certainly, **madam**."
menu (n)★	/ˈmenjuː/	Speisekarte	Can we see the **menu**, please?
soup (n)★	/suːp/	Suppe	You usually eat **soup** at the start of a meal.
spider (n)	/ˈspaɪdə/	Spinne	A **spider** is a black or brown insect with eight legs that a lot of people are frightened of.
steak (n)	/steɪk/	Steak	The man orders **steak** and chips.
wave about (v)★★	/weɪv/	herumfuchteln mit	In the poem, the waiter tells the woman not to **wave** the spider about.
wrong (adj)★★★	/rɒŋ/	falsch	The waitress says they've got the **wrong** knives and forks.
young (adj)★★★	/jʌŋ/	jung	**Young** is the opposite of 'old'.

Culture: Teenage Life (pp. 66–7)

actually (adv)★★★	/ˈæktʊəli/	eigentlich	I like my parents – they're quite cool **actually**.
addictive (adj)	/əˈdɪktɪv/	süchtig machend	The Internet can be very **addictive**.
anywhere (adv)★★	/ˈeniweə/	(n)irgendwohin	I hate being 15 – you can't do anything, you can't go **anywhere**.
cool (adj)★★★	/kuːl/	cool	Amy thinks her parents are quite **cool**.
definitely (adv)★★	/ˈdefɪnɪtli/	bestimmt	There are **definitely** loads of girls who go on diets when they don't need to.
designer clothes (n pl)	/dɪˌzaɪnə ˈkləʊðz/	Designer-Kleidung	A lot of teenagers think it's important to wear **designer clothes**.
diet (n)★★	/ˈdaɪət/	Diät; Schlankheitskur	People go on **diets** when they think they're too fat and need to lose weight.
disco (n)	/ˈdɪskəʊ/	Disko	Do you enjoy going to **discos**?

exam (n)★★	/ɪgˈzæm/	Prüfung	Helen wants to become a model after she's done her **exams**.
guy (n)★★	/gaɪ/	Typ; Kerl	I'd like to meet a nice **guy** and maybe get married.
kid (n)★★	/kɪd/	Kind	Jessie thinks people treat teenagers like **kids**.
loads of ...★★	/ˈləʊdz əv/	viele; eine Menge	**Loads of** girls go on diets when they're teenagers.
marriage (n)★★★	/ˈmærɪdʒ/	Heiraten; Ehe	**Marriage**? Well, one day perhaps.
model (n)★★★	/ˈmɒdl/	Model	A **model** is a person whose job is to show clothes by wearing them.
obsessive (adj)	/əbˈsesɪv/	wie besessen	Some girls get very upset and **obsessive** about their weight.
organise (v)★★	/ˈɔːgənaɪz/	organisieren	They **organise** a disco for all the schools but it's rubbish.
percentage (n)★	/pəˈsentɪdʒ/	Prozentsatz	What **percentage** of teenagers do you think are happy?
responsibility (n)★★★	/rɪspɒnsɪˈbɪlɪti/	Verantwortung	One of the advantages of being a teenager is that you don't have any real **responsibilities**.
spend (money) (v)★★★	/spend/	Geld ausgeben	How much do teenagers **spend** on mobile phones a month?
survey (n)★★	/ˈsɜːveɪ/	Umfrage	Teenagers were asked to answer questions about their lifestyle in a recent **survey**.
teenager (n)★	/ˈtiːneɪdʒə/	Teenager; Jugendliche(r)	A **teenager** is someone aged between 13 and 19.
total (adj)★★★	/ˈtəʊtəl/	ganz	20% of the **total** population think it is important to wear designer clothes.
treat (v)★★★	/triːt/	behandeln	Stop **treating** us like kids!
trust (v)★★	/trʌst/	vertrauen	A lot of parents don't **trust** their teenage children.
unhappy (adj)★★	/ʌnˈhæpi/	unglücklich	If you're upset you feel stressed and **unhappy**.
upset (adj)★	/ʌpˈset/	ärgerlich; durcheinander; geknickt	Why are you so **upset**?

Unit 6

1 Have you recorded everything? (pp. 68–9)

animal (n)★★★	/ˈænɪməl/	Tier	There are lots of wild **animals** in Richmond Park, including red deer.
bear (n)	/beə/	Bär	A **bear** is a large, heavy animal with brown or black fur.
bird (n)★★★	/bɜːd/	Vogel	You can see ducks and other **birds** in the Serpentine Lake.
break (v)★★★	/breɪk/	kaputtmachen	Be careful! Don't **break** the camera.
conversation (n)★★★	/kɒnvəˈseɪʃən/	Gespräch	The camera can film people and record **conversations**.
cow (n)★★	/kaʊ/	Kuh	A **cow** is a black, brown or white farm animal that gives us milk and meat.
deer (n)	/dɪə/	Rehe; Rotwild; Damwild	**Deer** are shy animals.

duck (n)	/dʌk/	Ente	There are **ducks** and other wild birds on the lake.
email (n)★★★	/ˈiːmeɪl/	Email	Send me an **email** to tell me how you are.
farm (n)	/fɑːm/	(Bauern)hof; landwirtschaftlicher Betrieb	London has several city **farms** where you can see sheep, pigs, cows and goats.
friendly (adj)★★	/ˈfrendli/	freundlich	"Has Carol been **friendly** to Jack?" "No, she hasn't."
giraffe (n)	/dʒɪˈrɑːf/	Giraffe	**Giraffes** are tall animals with long necks.
go back (to) (phr v)	/gəʊ ˈbæk (tə)/	zurückgehen	It's late – we should **go back** to the hotel.
goat (n)	/gəʊt/	Ziege	A **goat** is a farm animal that has small horns and gives us milk.
hippo (n)	/ˈhɪpəʊ/	Flusspferd; Nilpferd	A **hippo** is a large animal with thick skin that lives in rivers and lakes in Africa.
horrible (adj)★	/ˈhɒrɪbəl/	gemein	I have tried to talk to her but she's been **horrible** to me.
horse (n)★★★	/hɔːs/	Pferd	Can you ride a **horse**?
joke (v)	/dʒəʊk/	scherzen	I'm not **joking**, Jack – Carol likes you a lot.
lion (n)	/ˈlaɪən/	Löwe	A **lion** is a very large animal with brown fur that people call 'King of the Jungle'.
in the middle of★★★	/ɪn ðə ˈmɪdl əv/	mitten in	The Serpentine Lake is **in the middle of** Hyde Park.
monkey (n)	/ˈmʌŋki/	Affe	**Monkeys** live in trees and move around very quickly.
open space (n)	/ˈəʊpən ˈspeɪs/	offene Fläche; freier Raum	London has more parks and **open spaces** than most other large cities.
pig (n)★	/pɪg/	Schwein	**Pigs** are large pink farm animals that give us meat.
planet (n)★	/ˈplænɪt/	Planet	The **planet** that we all live on is called Earth.
protect (v)★★★	/prəˈtekt/	schützen	The Zoo works hard to **protect** animals that are in danger.
pull someone's leg	/ˌpʊl sʌmwʌnz ˈleg/	jmd auf den Arm nehmen	"She really likes you." "You're **pulling my leg** – she hasn't said a word to me all day."
sheep (n)★★	/ʃiːp/	Schaf	A **sheep** is a farm animal with a white coat that we use to make wool.
have a shower (n)	/hæv ə ˈʃaʊə/	duschen	I usually **have a shower** before breakfast.
sound (n)★★★	/saʊnd/	Ton	This camera has fantastic **sound** so you can hear what people are saying.
species (n)★★	/ˈspiːʃiːz/	Spezies	There are many different **species** of animal in London Zoo.
squirrel (n)	/ˈskwɪrəl/	Eichhörnchen	There are lots of **squirrels** in Hyde Park.
tiger (n)	/ˈtaɪgə/	Tiger	**Tigers** are very large cats with orange and black stripes.
wild (adj)★★	/waɪld/	wild	Richmond Park has lots of **wild** animals, including large numbers of deer.
wildlife (n)	/ˈwaɪldlaɪf/	Tierwelt	The Zoo tries to protect **wildlife** that is in danger.
work out (phr v)	/ˌwɜːk ˈaʊt/	herausbekommen	Have you **worked out** how to use the camera?

2 Have you ever ...? (pp. 70–71)

annoyed (adj)★★	/əˈnɔɪd/	verärgert	Carol was really **annoyed**. I've never seen anyone so angry before.
bus driver (n)	/bʌs ˌdraɪvə/	Busfahrer	We paid the **bus driver** as we got on the bus.
bus station (n)	/bʌs ˌsteɪʃən/	Busbahnhof	How long did you have to wait at the **bus station**?
bus stop (n)	/bʌs stɒp/	Bushaltestelle	There was a queue of people waiting at the **bus stop**.
bus ticket (n)	/bʌs ˌtɪkɪt/	Busfahrkarte	We bought our **bus tickets** from the driver.
bus timetable (n)	/bʌs ˌtaɪmteɪbəl/	Busfahrplan	The **bus timetable** says there are three buses to Cambridge every hour.
car driver (n)	/kɑː ˌdraɪvə/	Autofahrer	**Car drivers** get annoyed when there's too much traffic.
car engine (n)	/kɑː(r) ˌendʒɪn/	(Auto)motor	Make sure there's enough oil in the **car engine**.
car park (n)	/kɑː pɑːk/	Parkplatz	The **car park's** full.
cheer up (phr v)	/tʃɔː(r) ˈʌp/	Nun lach doch mal!	Hey, **cheer up**! It's not the end of the world.
electric (adj)★	/ɪˈlektrɪk/	elektrisch	How old is the world's first **electric** underground railway?
embarrassed (adj)★	/ɪmˈbærəst/	verlegen	Jack feels **embarrassed** because Carol heard his conversation with Sally.
guidebook (n)	/ˈgaɪdbʊk/	Reiseführer	Carol read about the London Transport Museum in the **guidebook**.
railway engine (n)★★★	/ˈreɪlweɪ ˌendʒɪn/	Lokomotive	You can see old **railway engines** in the London Transport Museum.
railway line (n)	/ˈreɪlweɪ laɪn/	Schiene; Gleis	Parts of the **railway line** need to be repaired.
railway station (n)	/ˈreɪlweɪ ˌsteɪʃən/	Bahnhof	Meet me at the **railway station** at 3 o'clock.
simulator (n)	/ˈsɪmjʊleɪtə/	Simulator	You can practise train driving on the **simulator**.
traffic (n)★★★	/ˈtræfɪk/	Verkehr	Buses move slowly because there is too much **traffic**.
train driver (n)★★★	/treɪn ˌdraɪvə/	Lokführer	The **train driver** was responsible for the accident.
train station (n)	/treɪn ˌsteɪʃən/	Bahnhof	What time do you arrive at the **train station**?
train ticket (n)	/treɪn ˌtɪkɪt/	Zugfahrkarte	How much is a **train ticket** to Oxford?
train timetable (n)	/treɪn ˌtaɪmteɪbəl/	Zugfahrplan	The **train timetable** will tell you what time the train leaves.
tube (n)★	/tjuːb/	U-Bahn	I know! We're in the **tube**. Why don't we make a video about the underground?

3 Too many tourists (pp. 72–3)

balloon (n)	/bəˈluːn/	Ballon	**Balloons** were floating in the air above the stadium.
channel (n)★★	/ˈtʃænəl/	Kanäle; Programme	Greg has satellite TV at home with 54 **channels**.
drive (v)★★★	/draɪv/	fahren	Are you old enough to **drive**?
empty (adj)★★★	/ˈemti/	leer	There was nobody in the shop – it was completely **empty**!
grass (n)★★★	/grɑːs/	Gras	Cows and sheep were eating the **grass**.
musical (n)	/ˈmjuːzɪkəl/	Musical	Mamma Mia! is a very successful **musical**.

musician (n)★	/mjuːˈzɪʃən/	Musiker	Madame Tussaud's is full of models of famous people, including singers and **musicians**.
make a noise★★★	/meɪk ə ˈnɔɪz/	Sei ganz leise!	Listen carefully and don't **make a noise**.
queue (n)★	/kjuː/	Warteschlange	A **queue** is a long line of people waiting for something.
satellite TV (n)	/ˌsætəlaɪt tiː ˈviː/	Satelliten-Fernsehen	On **satellite TV** you can get lots of channels.
sight (n)★★★	/saɪt/	Sehenswürdigkeiten	When people visit London they want to see all the **sights**.

4 Integrated skills/Favourite places (pp. 74–5)

airport (n)★★★	/ˈeəpɔːt/	Flughafen	Take a bus from the **airport** to get to the Iguazú Falls.
angel (n)★★	/ˈeɪndʒəl/	Engel	The statue in Picture C is called 'The **Angel** of the North'.
border (n)★★	/ˈbɔːdə/	Grenze	The Iguazú Falls are on the **border** between Argentina and Brazil.
create (v)★★★	/kriˈeɪt/	schaffen; kreieren	The Cristo Redentor statue was **created** by a French artist, Paul Landowski.
ferry boat (n)	/ˈferi bəʊt/	Fähre	The trip across the water on the **ferry boat** takes twenty minutes.
halfway (adv)	/hɑːfˈweɪ/	den halben Weg	You can go **halfway** up the statue in a lift.
hard (adj)★★★	/hɑːd/	hart	Walking to the top of the Eiffel Tower is **hard** work!
hear of (phr v)	/hɪə(r) əv/	hören von	Not many people have **heard of** the town of Agrigento in Sicily.
lift (n)★	/lɪft/	Lift; Aufzug; Fahrstuhl	A **lift** takes you halfway up the statue.
mountain (n)★★★	/ˈmaʊntɪn/	Berg	The Cristo Redentor statue is on top of the Corcovado **mountain** in Rio.
pillar (n)	/ˈpɪlə/	Säule	The **pillars** of the Temple of Concord are 40 metres tall.
reason (n)★★★	/ˈriːzən/	Grund	The real **reason** people go to the Eiffel Tower is that there's a fantastic view from the top.
right-hand (adj)	/raɪt hænd/	rechte Seite	Sit on the **right-hand** side of the train as you go up the mountain because the view is better.
side (n)★★★	/saɪd/	Seite	The train climbed slowly up the **side** of the mountain.
statue (n)	/ˈstætʃuː/	Statue	The **statue** is 46 metres high.
steep (adj)★	/stiːp/	steil	The side of the mountain is very **steep** and there's a fabulous view as you go up on the train.
temple (n)	/ˈtempəl/	Tempel	The **Temple** of Concord is the best Greek temple in the world.
waterfalls (n pl)	/ˈwɔːtəfɔːlz/	Wasserfälle	The **waterfalls** are two kilometres long!
the whole of …★★★	/ðə ˈhəʊl əv/	ganz	You can see **the whole of** Paris from the top of the Eiffel Tower.
world-famous (adj)	/wɜːld ˈfeɪməs/	weltberühmt	The Statue of Liberty is a **world-famous** monument.

Inspiration *Extra!* (pp. 76–7)

painting (n)★★	/ˈpeɪntɪŋ/	Malerei; Mal-	Jenny Dixon won a **painting** competition and the prize was a weekend in New York.
passport (n)★	/ˈpɑːspɔːt/	(Reise)pass	When Jenny arrived in New York she couldn't find her **passport** and took the next plane home.

Review Units 5–6 (pp. 78–9)

audience (n)★★★	/ˈɔːdiəns/	Publikum	At the Sydney Olympic Games she sang to a worldwide TV **audience** of four billion people.
award (n)★★	/əˈwɔːd/	Auszeichnung	Kylie has won hundreds of **awards**.
billion	/ˈbɪljən/	Milliarde; Billion	She sang to a TV audience of four **billion** people.
hit (n)★	/hɪt/	Hit; Schlager	Locomotion was a Number One **hit** in Australia.
household name (n)	/ˌhaʊshəʊld ˈneɪm/	jedem ein Begriff	Kylie Minogue is a **household name** around the world.
single (n)	/ˈsɪŋgəl/	Single	What was the name of Kylie's first **single**?
worldwide (adj)	/ˈwɜːldwaɪd/	weltweit	A **worldwide** TV audience of four billion people watched her at the Sydney Olympics.

Unit 7

1 They must eat insects and worms (pp. 80–81)

alone (adv)★★	/əˈləʊn/	allein	It must be frightening to spend the whole night **alone** in the jungle.
autograph (n)	/ˈɔːtəgrɑːf/	Autogramm	Don't ask the actors for their **autographs**!
basic (adj)★★★	/ˈbeɪsɪk/	wesentlich; grundsätzlich	The group gets **basic** things like knives and forks.
beans (n pl)	/biːnz/	Bohnen	**Beans** are vegetables that contain a lot of protein.
bite (n)	/baɪt/	Biss	Snake **bites** can kill you.
box of matches (n)	/bɒks əv ˈmætʃɪz/	Schachtel Streichhölzer	We need to light a fire. Has anyone got a **box of matches**?
camp (n)★★	/kæmp/	Lager	The celebrities live together in a **camp** in the jungle.
candle (n)	/ˈkændəl/	Kerze	We had no electricity so we had to use **candles**.
celebrity (n)★	/səˈlebrɪti/	VIP; berühmte Persönlichkeit	**Celebrities** are people who are famous.
charity (n)★★	/ˈtʃærəti/	Wohltätigkeitszwecke	The last person left wins a lot of money for **charity**.

Word	Pronunciation	German	Example
chopping board (n)	/ˈtʃɒpɪŋ bɔːd/	Schneidebrett	Cut up the vegetables on a **chopping board**.
clap (v)	/klæp/	klatschen	You **clap** by hitting your hands together to show that you admire or enjoy something.
complain (v)★★★	/kəmˈpleɪn/	sich beschweren	They **complain** that they are bored and hungry.
contact (n)★★★	/ˈkɒntækt/	Kontakt	They have no **contact** with the outside world.
contestant (n)	/kənˈtestənt/	Teilnehmer; Kandidat	In the second week viewers decide which **contestants** must leave the jungle.
cook (v)★★★	/kʊk/	kochen	The celebrities must **cook** their own food.
cooking pot (n)	/ˈkʊkɪŋ pɒt/	Kochtopf	A **cooking pot** is a large metal container used for cooking food.
crocodile (n)	/ˈkrɒkədaɪl/	Krokodil	**Crocodiles** are large, dangerous animals with sharp teeth that live in water.
danger (n)★★★	/ˈdeɪndʒə/	Gefahr	Don't forget the **dangers** of the jungle!
during (prep)★★★	/ˈdʒʊərɪŋ/	während	**During** the time they spend in the jungle, hidden cameras film everything they do.
equipment (n)★★★	/ɪˈkwɪpmənt/	Geräte	There's a lot of expensive **equipment** in the studio – please don't touch it.
film crew (n)	/ˈfɪlm kruː/	Kameraleute	Celebrities only see the show's presenters and **film crew**.
flash photograph (n)	/ˌflæʃ ˈfəʊtəɡrɑːf/	Blitzlichtfoto	A **flash photograph** is one you take when it is dark using a special light.
fortnight (n)	/ˈfɔːtnaɪt/	vierzehn Tage	A **fortnight** is a period of time equivalent to two weeks.
fortunately (adv)★	/ˈfɔːtʃənətli/	glücklicherweise	**Fortunately** the largest crocodile was plastic!
give up (phr v)	/ɡɪv ˈʌp/	aufgeben	It's not easy to **give up** luxuries and spend a fortnight in the jungle.
hidden camera (n)	/ˌhɪdn ˈkæmrə/	versteckte Kamera	**Hidden cameras** film everything they do and say.
hide (v)★★★	/haɪd/	verstecken	You **hide** something when you do not want other people to see or find it.
insect (n)★	/ˈɪnsekt/	Insekt	The contestants must do things like eat **insects** and worms.
item (n)★★★	/ˈaɪtəm/	Gegenstand	**Items** such as notebooks or make-up are considered luxuries.
jungle (n)	/ˈdʒʌŋɡəl/	Dschungel	A **jungle** is a large area in a hot country where lots of trees and plants grow close together.
litter (n)	/ˈlɪtə/	Abfälle	**Litter** is paper or bags that people drop on the floor.
live (adj)★	/laɪv/	lebend	Carrying a **live** snake is a dangerous thing to do.
log (n)	/lɒɡ/	Holzscheit	A **log** is a piece of wood that you cut for a fire.
log fire (n)	/lɒɡ ˈfaɪə/	Holzfeuer	There is a **log fire** at the centre of the camp.
luxury (n)	/ˈlʌkʃəri/	Luxus	Each person can take one '**luxury**' such as a hat, a notebook or make-up.
make-up (n)	/ˈmeɪk ʌp/	Make-up	Women put **make-up** on their face to make themselves look more beautiful.

match (n)★★★	/mætʃ/	Streichholz	She lit a fire with a **match**.
mirror (n)★★	/ˈmɪrə/	Spiegel	A **mirror** is a piece of glass used for looking at yourself in.
No entry	/ˌnəʊ ˈentri/	Zutritt verboten	'**No entry**' is a sign that stops people going into a place.
outside world (n)	/aʊtsaɪd ˈwɜːld/	Außenwelt	It's hard not having any contact with the **outside world**.
paraffin (n)	/ˈpærəfɪn/	Petroleum; Paraffin	**Paraffin** is a type of oil used for lighting fires.
poisonous (adj)	/ˈpɔɪzənəs/	giftig	Snakes are **poisonous** animals that can kill you.
reality TV show (n)	/rɪˈæləti tiː ˈviː ʃəʊ/	Reality-TV-Show	**Reality TV shows** are very popular nowadays.
rhino (rhinocerous) (n)	/ˈraɪnəʊ/	Nashorn	A **rhino** is a large animal from Africa or Asia with thick skin and a horn on its nose.
shampoo (n)	/ʃæmˈpuː/	Shampoo	You wash your hair using **shampoo**.
smoke (v)★★	/sməʊk/	rauchen	Don't **smoke** inside the building!
snake (n)	/sneɪk/	Schlange	A **snake** is a long, thin animal that moves along the ground and has a poisonous bite.
spoon (n)★	/spuːn/	Löffel	You eat soup with a **spoon**.
supplies (n pl)★★★	/səˈplaɪz/	Ausrüstung; Vorräte; Proviant	Basic **supplies** such as spoons, matches and toilet paper are given to the group.
survival technique (n)	/səˈvaɪvəl tekˌniːk/	Überlebenstechniken	You need some basic **survival techniques** to survive in the jungle.
take part	/teɪk ˈpɑːt/	teilnehmen	The celebrities who **take part** in the programme must live in the jungle without any luxuries.
task (n)★★★	/tɑːsk/	Aufgabe	Every day a celebrity must do a special **task** in order to get more food.
toilet paper (n)	/ˈtɔɪlət peɪpə/	Toilettenpapier	Basic supplies include **toilet paper** and shampoo.
touch (v)★★★	/tʌtʃ/	berühren; anfassen	Don't **touch** the equipment!
treatment (n)★★★	/ˈtriːtmənt/	Behandlung	Emergency **treatment** of snake bites is a basic survival technique.
viewer (n)	/ˈvjuːə/	Zuschauer	TV **viewers** choose who does the special task each day.
visit (n)★★★	/ˈvɪzɪt/	Besuch	Enjoy your **visit** to YTV!
worm (n)	/wɜːm/	Wurm	**Worms** are long, thin animals that live in soil.

2 Do we have to go? (pp. 82–3)

ages (n pl)★★★	/ˈeɪdʒɪz/	eine Ewigkeit	Do we have to go? Last time we had to stay there for **ages**.
care (v)★★★	/keə/	einem was bedeuten	"You'll miss something really exciting." "I don't **care**. I have to do some shopping."
catch (a train/bus) (v)★★★	/kætʃ (ə treɪn,bʌs)/	nehmen; kriegen	You must buy a ticket when you **catch** a bus or train.
check-out (n)	/ˈtʃekaʊt/	Kasse	We had to queue for ages at the **check-out** to pay.

clean (v)★★★	/kliːn/	sauber machen	I **clean** my room once a week.
clearly (adv)★★★	/ˈklɪəli/	deutlich	Write **clearly** with a black pen.
details (n pl)★★★	/ˈdiːteɪlz/	Details	For the rest of you, here are the **details** of this afternoon's visit.
enter (a competition) (v)★★★	/ˈentə (ə kɒmpəˈtɪʃən)/	sich melden	You pay £5 to **enter** the competition.
do the ironing	/ˌduː ðiː ˈaɪənɪŋ/	bügeln	When you **do the ironing** you make clothes that you have washed smooth, using an iron
the law (n)★★★	/ðə lɔː/	das Gesetz	**The law** says you have to wear a seat belt in a car.
lay the table	/ˌleɪ ðə ˈteɪbəl/	den Tisch decken	**Laying the table** means putting knives, forks, plates etc on it before a meal.
make your bed	/ˌmeɪk jɔː ˈbed/	das Bett machen	You **make your bed** in the morning after you have slept in it.
pass (an exam) (v)★★★	/ˌpɑːs (ən ɪgˈzæm)/	bestehen	You have to **pass** an exam before you can go to university.
put away (phr v)	/pʊt əˈweɪ/	wegräumen	Please **put** everything **away** in the cupboards.
seat belt (n)	/ˈsiːt belt/	Sicherheitsgurt	You have to wear a **seat belt** when you're in a car.
sentence (n)★★★	/ˈsentəns/	Satz	A **sentence** begins with a capital letter and ends with a full stop.
do the shopping	/ˌduː ðə ˈʃɒpɪŋ/	einkaufen	They've gone to the supermarket to **do the shopping**.
special effects (n pl)	/ˈspeʃl ɪˈfekts/	Trickaufnahmen; Specialeffect	Today we're going to see how they make **special effects** for films like *The Matrix*.
take-off (n)	/ˈteɪk ɒf/	Start; Abflug	Be at the airport an hour before **take-off**.
on time	/ɒn ˈtaɪm/	pünktlich	You must be **on time** for your lessons.
do the washing up	/ˌduː ðə wɒʃɪŋ ˈʌp/	spülen; abwaschen	After the meal Ben and Carol **did the washing up**.

3 Don't be frightened! (pp. 84–5)

alive (adj)★★★	/əˈlaɪv/	lebendig	The dinosaurs come **alive** in our exciting animated display.
amazed (adj)	/əˈmeɪzd/	erstaunt	We were **amazed** to see the animated dinosaurs.
amazing (adj)★	/əˈmeɪzɪŋ/	erstaunlich	What an **amazing** exhibition!
amongst (prep)★★★	/əˈmʌŋst/	unter	Experience the danger of life **amongst** the dinosaurs that lived on our planet for 160 million years.
amphibian (n)	/æmˈfɪbiən/	Amphibie	**Amphibians** are animals that live on land and in water.
animated display (n)	/ˌænɪmeɪtɪd dɪˈspleɪ/	Animation; animierte Darstellung	See the dinosaurs come alive in our **animated display**.
baby (n)★★★	/ˈbeɪbi/	Baby	Mammals feed their **babies** with milk.
brain (n)★★	/breɪn/	Gehirn	If you want to understand how the **brain** works, visit the 'Human biology' exhibition.

creature (n)★★	/ˈkriːtʃə/	Lebewesen	Some sea **creatures** live so deep they have to provide their own light.
deep (adj)★★★	/diːp/	tief	They live so **deep** they have to provide their own light.
develop (v)★★★	/dɪˈveləp/	sich entwickeln	Understand how your mind and body grow and **develop**.
dinosaur (n)	/ˈdaɪnəsɔː/	Dinosaurier	**Dinosaurs** are now extinct.
earthquake (n)	/ˈɜːθkweɪk/	Erdbeben	The volcano erupted, causing an **earthquake**.
environment (n)★★★	/ɪnˈvaɪrənmənt/	Umwelt	We are all responsible for looking after our **environment**.
erupt (v)	/ɪˈrʌpt/	ausbrechen	When a volcano **erupts**, hot liquid and steam come out of it.
eruption (n)	/ɪˈrʌpʃən/	Ausbruch	When a volcano erupts, we call this a volcanic **eruption**.
excited (adj)★★	/ɪkˈsaɪtɪd/	aufgeregt	They were **excited** about seeing the dinosaur exhibition.
experience (v)★★★	/ɪkˈspɪəriəns/	erfahren	**Experience** the sights and sounds of a rainforest!
extinct (adj)	/ɪkˈstɪŋkt/	ausgestorben	Animals that are **extinct** no longer live on our planet.
extraordinary (adj)★	/ɪkˈstrɔːdənri/	erstaunlich; sonderbar	Dinosaurs were **extraordinary** animals that lived on Earth for 160 million years.
fascinated (adj)	/ˈfæsɪneɪtɪd/	fasziniert	The children were **fascinated** by the dinosaur exhibition.
fascinating (adj)★	/ˈfæsɪneɪtɪŋ/	faszinierend	'Earth today and tomorrow' is a **fascinating** exhibition showing how living things interact with each other.
feather (n)	/ˈfeðə/	Feder; Gefieder	Birds have two wings and **feathers**.
feed (v)★★★	/fiːd/	ernähren	Mammals **feed** their babies with milk.
frightened (adj)★	/ˈfraɪtnd/	Angst haben vor	Are you **frightened** of snakes?
frightening (adj)★	/ˈfraɪtnɪŋ/	beängstigend	The earthquake simulator was really **frightening**.
grow (v)★★★	/grəʊ/	wachsen	Test your mind and body and understand how they **grow** and develop.
highlight (n)	/ˈhaɪlaɪt/	Höhepunkt	These exhibitions are just a few **highlights** of the Natural History Museum.
human being (n)★★	/ˌhjuːmən ˈbiːɪŋ/	Mensch	**Human beings** are changing the environment.
intelligent (adj)★★	/ɪnˈtelɪdʒənt/	intelligent	Human beings are the most **intelligent** form of life on the planet.
interact (v)	/ɪntəˈrækt/	interagieren; aufeneinander wirken	'Earth today and tomorrow' shows how living things **interact** with each other.
interactive (adj)	/ɪntəˈræktɪv/	interaktiv	'Human biology' is a highly **interactive** exhibition.
lay eggs	/leɪ ˈegz/	Eier legen	Reptiles and birds both **lay eggs**.
mammal (n)	/ˈmæməl/	Säugetier	Human beings are the most intelligent **mammal** in the world.
mind (n)★★★	/maɪnd/	Verstand	Test your **mind** and body in the highly interactive exhibition.
power (n)★★★	/ˈpaʊə/	Stärke; Kraft;Wucht	The **power** of an earthquake is frightening!
provide (v)★★★	/prəˈvaɪd/	liefern; schaffen	These sea creatures live so deep they have to **provide** their own light.
rainforest (n)	/ˈreɪnfɒrɪst/	Regenwald	A **rainforest** is a very thick forest in a tropical area where it rains a lot.

rather (I'd rather ...)★★★	/ˈrɑːðə/	lieber	"I'd **rather** see the Dinosaurs exhibition." "Oh no! I'm tired of dinosaurs!"
reptile (n)	/ˈreptaɪl/	Reptil	Snakes, crocodiles and tortoises are all types of **reptile**.
shocking (adj)	/ˈʃɒkɪŋ/	erschütternd	Find out how **shocking** an earthquake feels in our earthquake simulator.
surprising (adj)★★	/səˈpraɪzɪŋ/	erstaunlich	The exhibition is full of **surprising** fish, amphibians and reptiles.
test (v)★★★	/test/	testen	**Test** your mind and body in the 'Human biology' exhibition.
thrill (n)	/θrɪl/	Reiz; Nervenkitzel	Experience the **thrill** and danger of life amongst the dinosaurs!
tiring (adj)	/ˈtaɪərɪŋ/	ermüdend	Walking round the shops all day is **tiring**.
tortoise (n)	/ˈtɔːtəs/	Schildkröte	A **tortoise** is a reptile with a hard shell that moves very slowly.
volcano (n)	/vɒlˈkeɪnəʊ/	Vulkan	A **volcano** is a mountain with an opening at the top that hot liquid and steam come out of when it erupts.
water cycle (n)	/ˈwɔːtə saɪkəl/	Wasserzyklus	You can follow the **water cycle** on a huge video wall.

4 Integrated Skills: Describing a journey (pp. 86–7)

absolutely (adv)★	/ˈæbsəluːtli/	absolut	The Ice Globe is an **absolutely** stunning theatre.
advertisement (n)	/ədˈvɜːtɪsmənt/	Werbung; Reklame	Gill saw an **advertisement** for an eight-day trip to the Arctic and thought it was too good to miss!
bar (n)★	/bɑː/	Bar	The hotel has a **bar** made entirely of ice!
bedroom (n)★★	/ˈbedruːm/	Schlafzimmer	Guests sleep in ice **bedrooms**.
cross-country skiing (n)	/ˌkrɒs kʌntri ˈskiːɪŋ/	Langlaufski	Popular activities include travelling on sleds, **cross-country skiing** and snowmobile safaris.
culture (n)★★★	/ˈkʌltʃə/	Kultur	Tourists are now helping to keep the Sami **culture** alive.
exhausting (adj)	/ɪkˈzɔːstɪŋ/	erschöpfend	The trip across the Arctic was **exhausting**.
flash (v)★	/flæʃ/	aufblitzen	Watch the Northern Lights **flash** across the sky from the seats in the ice theatre.
freezing (adj)	/ˈfriːzɪŋ/	eiskalt	Most guests stay only one night at the Ice Hotel because it's **freezing**!
herd (n)	/hɜːd/	Herde	Today they also use snowmobiles to follow the reindeer **herds**.
herd (v)	/hɜːd/	treiben; hüten	If you **herd** animals you bring them together into a group.
husky (dog) (n)	/ˈhʌski (dɒg)/	Husky	Gill did an eight-day trip to the Arctic running a team of **husky** dogs.
ice (n)★★	/aɪs/	Eis	The world-famous **Ice** Hotel is built entirely of ice!
increased (adj)★★	/ɪnˈkriːst/	erhöht; gestiegen	The **increased** tourism in Lapland is helping to keep the Sami culture alive.
inhabitant (n)	/ɪnˈhæbɪtənt/	Bewohner; Einwohner	The original **inhabitants** of the region are called the Sami.
Lapland (n)	/ˈlæplænd/	Lappland	The Ice Hotel is in a region called **Lapland**.
major (adj)★★★	/ˈmeɪdʒə/	wichtig	The hotel has become a **major** tourist attraction.

means of transport (n)	/ˌmiːnz əv ˈtrænzpɔːt/	Transportmittel	The snowmobile is an important **means of transport** for the Sami people.
melt (v)★	/melt/	schmelzen	They have to rebuild the hotel every year because it **melts** in spring.
No way!	/ˌnəʊ ˈweɪ/	Niemals!	"Would you like to run a team of husky dogs in the Arctic?" "**No way!**"
original (adj)★★★	/əˈrɪdʒənəl/	Ur-; ursprünglich	The Sami people are the **original** inhabitants of the region.
raise (money) (v)★★★	/reɪz (mʌni)/	sammeln; auftreiben	How much money did Gill **raise** for charity?
reindeer (n)	/ˈreɪndɪə/	Renntier	The Sami people live by herding **reindeer**.
replica (n)	/ˈreplɪkə/	Nachbildung	The Ice Globe is a **replica** of the Globe Theatre in London!
sled (n)	/sled/	Schlitten	The Sami used to travel across the snow on **sleds** pulled by reindeer or huskies.
snow (n)★★	/snəʊ/	Schnee	Sleds are useful for travelling across **snow** or ice.
snowmobile (n)	/ˈsnəʊməbiːl/	Schneemobil	**Snowmobiles** are vehicles used for travelling across snow and ice.
spring (n)★★	/sprɪŋ/	Frühling	The hotel melts every **spring**!
stretch (v)★★	/stretʃ/	sich ausbreiten	Lapland is a region that **stretches** across four countries – Russia, Finland, Sweden and Norway.
stunning (adj)	/ˈstʌnɪŋ/	überwältigend; atemberaubend	The Ice Globe is a **stunning** theatre.
tourism (n)	/ˈtʊərɪzm/	Tourismus	The Ice Hotel has brought new life and increased **tourism** to Lapland.
tourist centre (n)	/ˈtʊərɪst sentə/	Touristikzentrum	Jukkasjärvi has become a popular **tourist centre**.
traditionally (adv)	/trəˈdɪʃnəli/	traditionell	**Traditionally** the Sami lived by herding reindeer.
tundra (n)	/ˈtʌndrə/	Tundra	They use sleds and snowmobiles to travel across the **tundra**.
version (n)★	/ˈvɜːʃən/	Version; Fassung	The first play was a 70-minute **version** of Hamlet.
wedding (n)★★	/ˈwedɪŋ/	Hochzeit	The ice church is very popular for **weddings**.
windy (adj)	/ˈwɪndi/	windig	The flight to Sweden was frightening because it was very **windy**.
worried (adj)★	/ˈwʌrɪd/	in Sorge; beunruhigt	Gill was **worried** because she's very frightened of flying.

Inspiration *Extra!* (pp. 88–9)

bathroom (n)★★	/ˈbɑːθruːm/	Badezimmer	The **bathroom** is the room where you wash and have a shower.
frown (n)	/fraʊn/	Stirnrunzeln	"Why did you think that I was extinct?" the dinosaur roared with a **frown**.
kitchen (n)★★★	/ˈkɪtʃɪn/	Küche	The **kitchen** is the room where you cook meals.
library (n)★★★	/ˈlaɪbrəri/	Bibliothek	A **library** is a place where people go to borrow books or where they can sit and read.
office (n)★★★	/ˈɒfɪs/	Büro	An **office** is a room or place where people sit and work.
roar (v)	/rɔː/	brüllen	When an animal such as a lion **roars**, it makes a very loud noise because it is angry.

sitting room (n)	/ˈsɪtɪŋ ruːm/	Wohnzimmer	A **sitting room** is a room where you relax, watch TV etc.
swimming pool (n)	/ˈswɪmɪŋ puːl/	Schwimmbecken	You shouldn't take cameras or electronic equipment into a **swimming pool**.

Culture: Do the right thing (pp. 90–91)

adult (n)★★★	/ˈædʌlt/	Erwachsener	In China, Japan and Korea young people don't usually start conversations with **adults**.
bacon (n)	/ˈbeɪkən/	Speck; Schinken	Eggs and **bacon** is supposed to be the traditional British breakfast.
bend (v)★★	/bend/	biegen	People in Japan bow a lot – that means they **bend** their body forward when they meet each other.
body language (n)	/ˈbɒdi læŋgwɪdʒ/	Körpersprache	We use **body language** as well as words to communicate with people.
bow (v)	/baʊ/	sich verbeugen	In the photo on p. 91 you can see two Japanese men **bowing** to each other.
comment (n)★★★	/ˈkɒment/	Kommentar	In Britain it's polite to respond and make **comments** during a conversation to show you're interested.
common (adj)★★★	/ˈkɒmən/	normal; gewöhnlich	In Japan it's quite **common** for people to stay silent when someone is talking to them.
communicate (v)★	/kəˈmjuːnɪkeɪt/	kommunizieren	We use both words and body language to **communicate** with people.
in contrast★★	/ˌɪn ˈkɒntrɑːst/	im Gegensatz zu	Americans, **in contrast** with the Japanese, encourage young people to start conversations.
cover (v)★★★	/ˈkʌvə/	verbergen	People **cover** their mouth in Japan when they smile or laugh.
date (n)★★★	/deɪt/	Rendezvous	Do girls and boys kiss on their first **date** in your country?
disagree (v)★	/dɪsəˈgriː/	nicht der gleichen Meinung sein	Australians are interested in people who **disagree** with them.
encourage (v)★★★	/ɪnˈkʌrɪdʒ/	ermuntern	Americans **encourage** young people to start conversations.
facial expression (n)	/ˈfeɪʃl ɪkˌspreʃən/	Gesichtsausdruck	Gestures and **facial expressions** are used to communicate with other people.
gesture (n)★	/ˈdʒestʃə/	Geste	A **gesture** is a movement you make with your head or other part of your body.
hug (v)	/hʌg/	drücken	If you **hug** someone, you put your arms round them.
interest (n)★★★	/ˈɪntrəst/	Interesse	In Western cultures people look each other in the eye to show **interest** and trust.
invite (v)★★★	/ɪnˈvaɪt/	einladen	In Britain, if someone **invites** you to their home, you should arrive a few minutes late.

meanwhile (adv)★	/ˈmiːnwaɪl/	andererseits	Men in the Arab world often hug and kiss each other. **Meanwhile**, in Japan, people bow when they meet.
position (n)★★★	/pəˈzɪʃən/	Position	A 'superior' is someone who is in a higher social or work **position** than you.
respond (v)★★	/rɪsˈpɒnd/	antworten	In Britain we think that it is polite to **respond** when someone is talking to us.
stay silent (adj)★★	/ˈsaɪlənt/	still, ruhig, bleiben; schweigen	In parts of Northern Europe and Japan it's common for people to stay **silent** when someone is talking to them.
stare (v)★★	/steə/	anstarren	In Britain and the United States it isn't polite to **stare** at strangers.
superior (n)	/suˈpɪəriə/	Vorgesetzte(r)	Your boss is your '**superior**' because he/she is in a higher position than you.
table manners (n pl)	/ˈteɪbəl mænəz/	Tischmanieren	**Table manners** are how you behave and what you do when you are eating a meal.
take off (phr v)	/teɪk ˈɒf/	ausziehen	Do guests **take off** their shoes when they visit someone's house in your country?
thoughtfully (adv)	/ˈθɔːtfəli/	nachdenklich; aufmerksam	Indians often look long and **thoughtfully** at people they do not know.
trust (n)★★	/trʌst/	Vertrauen	People look each other in the eye in Western cultures to show interest and **trust**.
unfriendly (adj)	/ʌnˈfrendli/	unfreundlich	Sometimes Americans think Australians are rude and **unfriendly**.
Western (adj)★★	/ˈwestən/	westlich	There are a lot of differences in behaviour between **Western** cultures and Asian countries.

Unit 8

1 The characters seem to speak (pp. 92–3)

animation (n)	/æniˈmeɪʃən/	Animation	The quality of **animation** in the films is superb.
animator (n)	/ˈænimeitə/	Animator(in)	The **animator** uses the 'storyboard' to plan the film in detail.
argue (v)★★★	/ˈɑːgjuː/	sich streiten	Carol told Jack and Ben to stop **arguing**.
background (n)★★	/ˈbækgraʊnd/	Hintergrund	The **background** is planned by the designer.
blow (v)★★	/bləʊ/	pfeifen	The referee **blew** the whistle to signal the end of the match.
computer expert (n)	/kəmˈpjuːtə(r) ˌekspɜːt/	Computerfachmann	A **computer expert** is good at designing or repairing computers.
designer (n)★	/dɪˈzaɪnə/	Designer	They make a model of each character and the **designer** plans the background.

in detail ★★★	/ˌɪn ˈdiːteɪl/	detailliert; in allen Einzelheiten	The animator uses the storyboard to plan the film **in detail**.
film-maker (n)	/ˈfɪlmmeɪkə/	Filmemacher	It can take **film-makers** years to make a whole animated film.
inventor (n)	/ɪnˈventə/	Erfinder	Wallace is an **inventor** who loves eating cheese.
journalist (n) ★★	/ˈdʒɜːnəlɪst/	Journalist	**Journalists** write articles for newspapers and magazines.
manage to do sth	/ˈmænɪdʒ tə ˈduː sʌmθɪŋ/	es schaffen	Often the film-makers only **manage to** shoot three seconds of film a day.
millimetre (mm) (n)	/ˈmɪlimiːtə/	Millimeter	David and Peter learnt to make animated films using a 16 **mm** camera.
model (n) ★★★	/ˈmɒdəl/	Modell	They make a **model** of each character.
musician (n) ★	/mjuːˈzɪʃən/	Musiker	My ambition is to become a professional **musician**.
offer (v) ★★★	/ˈɒfə/	anbieten	The BBC **offered** to buy one of their first films.
pilot (n) ★	/ˈpaɪlət/	Pilot	**Pilots** fly aeroplanes.
plan (v) ★★★	/plæn/	planen	They **plan** the film in detail using a 'storyboard'.
process (n) ★★★	/ˈprəʊses/	Prozess; Verfahren	Making an animated film is a very slow **process**.
referee (n)	/refəˈriː/	Schiedsrichter	The **referee** blew the whistle at the end of the game.
refuse (v) ★★★	/rɪˈfjuːz/	sich weigern	Carol **refused** to dance with Ben.
save (v) ★★★	/seɪv/	retten	A lifebelt is used to **save** someone in the water.
schoolboy (n)	/ˈskuːlbɔɪ/	Schuljunge	The story started when two **schoolboys**, David Sproxton and Peter Lord, learnt to make animated films.
storyboard (n)	/ˈstɔːrɪbɔːd/	Storyboard; (bildliche Darstellung der Handlungsabläufe)	The '**storyboard**' consists of a series of pictures of the film.
text message (n)	/ˈtekst mesɪdʒ/	SMS-Nachricht	You use a mobile phone to send a **text message**.
tourist guide (n)	/ˈtʊərɪst gaɪd/	Reiseleiter; Fremdenführer	If you became a **tourist guide**, you could use your languages.
whistle (n)	/ˈwɪsəl/	Pfeife	The referee blew the **whistle** to signal the end of the match.

2 If you like a boy ... (pp. 94–5)

brightness (n)	/ˈbraɪtnəs/	Helligkeit	Each pixel records the **brightness** of the light.
button (n) ★★	/ˈbʌtən/	Knopf	To take a photo just press the **button**.
calculation (n) ★★	/ˌkælkjəˈleɪʃən/	Kalkulation	If you make **calculations** you use mathematics to work out answers.
compare (v)	/kəmˈpeə/	vergleichen	The computer **compares** what each pixel 'sees' with the other pixels around it.
computer chip (n)	/kəmˈpjuːtə tʃɪp/	Computerchip	Digital cameras don't use a film – instead they use a **computer chip**.
depressed (adj) ★	/dɪˈprest/	deprimiert	When I'm on my own, I get **depressed**.

digital photo (n)★	/ˌdɪdʒɪtəl ˈfəʊtəʊ/	Digitalfoto	**Digital photos** are in colour.
down (adj)★★★	/daʊn/	niedergeschlagen	I get depressed, you know, really **down** when I'm on my own.
feeling (n)★★★	/ˈfiːlɪŋ/	Gefühl	Carol finds it hard to show her **feelings**.
filter (n)	/fɪltə/	Filter	In a digital camera there is a **filter** in front of each pixel.
fortune teller (n)	/ˈfɔːtʃuːn ˌtelə/	Hellseher; Wahrsager(in)	**Fortune tellers** can judge people's characters by looking at the lines on their hand.
image (n)★★★	/ˈɪmɪdʒ/	Bild	When a digital camera records what it sees, it uses numbers not **images**.
information (n)★★★	/ɪnfəˈmeɪʃən/	Information	A digital camera records **information** as numbers.
mathematics (n)	/mæθəˈmætɪks/	Mathematik	If you use **mathematics** you use calculations to work out answers.
mean (= intend) (v)★★★	/miːn/	meinen; wollen	I've been rude to both of them. I didn't **mean** to be, but …
measure (v)★★★	/ˈmeʒə/	messen	Pixels **measure** light.
mix (v)★★	/mɪks/	mischen	If you **mix** red, green and blue light, you get white.
pixel (n)	/ˈpɪksəl/	Pixel	Digital cameras have a computer chip covered in **pixels**.
press (v)★★★	/pres/	drücken	Just **press** the button to take a picture.
primary colour (n)	/ˌpraɪməri ˈkʌlə/	Grundfarbe; Primärfarbe	Red, green and blue are the **primary colours**.
shout (v)★★★	/ʃaʊt/	(an)schreien	Carol told the fortune teller she had **shouted** at Greg.
square (n)★★★	/skweə/	Quadrat	A pixel is a **square** on a computer chip which measures light.
temper (n)	/ˈtempə/	Beherrschung (verlieren)	She loses her **temper** with bossy people.
tiny (adj)★★★	/ˈtaɪni/	winzig	The computer chip in a digital camera is covered in millions of **tiny** squares called pixels.

4 Integrated Skills: Describing a process (pp. 98–9)

bone (n)★★	/bəʊn/	Knochen	There are many dinosaur **bones** around the world.
bring to life	/brɪŋ tə ˈlaɪf/	zum Leben erwecken	The BBC TV series called *Walking With Dinosaurs* really **brings** dinosaurs **to life**.
CD player (n)	/siː ˈdiː pleɪə/	CD-Spieler	Has your car got a **CD player**?
colour (v)	/ˈkʌlə/	färben; anmalen	After making the white model we **coloured** the animal's skin.
contact (v)★★★	/ˈkɒntækt/	kontaktieren	You can use email to **contact** other learners of English.
DVD player (n)	/ˌdiː viː ˈdiː pleɪə/	DVD-Spieler	**DVD players** are replacing video recorders.
exist (v)★★★	/ɪgˈzɪst/	existieren	How can you film an animal which doesn't **exist**?
graded reader (n)	/ˌgreɪdɪd ˈriːdə/	nach Schwierigkeitsgrad gestufte Lektüre	A **graded reader** is a book written for people who have a particular level of English.
moon (n)★★	/muːn/	Mond	Dinosaurs lived in a world as real as ours, with a sun and a **moon**, day and night etc.

revise (v)	/rɪˈvaɪz/	revidieren; wiederholen	Look back through this book and **revise** what you have learnt.
scan (v)	/skæn/	scannen	**Scan** the image into the computer.
screen (n)★★	/skriːn/	Bildschirm	In *Walking With Dinosaurs* we see dinosaurs eating, running and fighting on our TV **screens**.
splash (v)	/splæʃ/	spritzen	The film crew moved things, **splashed** water, broke trees and so on – just like real dinosaurs.

Inspiration *Extra!* (pp. 100–101)

set (v)★★★	/set/	einstellen; setzen	**Set** the time and channel on the video recorder and press 'Record'.
video recorder (n)	/ˈvɪdɪəʊ rɪˌkɔːdə/	Videorecorder	Put the cassette in the **video recorder**.

Review Units 7–8 (pp. 102–3)

add (v)★★★	/æd/	addieren	When you **add** two and two you get four.
air travel (n)	/ˈeə trævəl/	Flugverkehr	The article on p. 102 is about **air travel** tips.
on average	/ɒn ˈævərɪdʒ/	im Durchschnitt	**On average** there are only 50 fatal accidents a year.
baggage (n)	/ˈbægɪdʒ/	Gepäck	Security checks and **baggage** X-rays can take a long time.
cheat (v)★	/tʃiːt/	mogeln; betrügen	You mustn't **cheat** and you mustn't send in more than one entry.
check (n)★★	/tʃek/	Check	Security **checks** can take a long time.
competitor (n)	/kəmˈpetɪtə/	Teilnehmer; Mitbewerber	**Competitors** under 16 must have their parents' permission.
enjoyable (adj)	/ɪnˈdʒɔɪəbəl/	angenehm	There are certain things you can do to make your journey safer and more **enjoyable**.
entry form (n)	/ˈentri fɔːm/	Anmeldeformular	Don't forget to sign your **entry form**.
fatal (adj)★	/ˈfeɪtəl/	tödlich	A **fatal** accident is one in which people are killed.
fit (adj)★	/fɪt/	fit; in Form	You need to take exercise if you want to keep **fit**.
ground (n)★★★	/graʊnd/	Boden	The **ground** was covered with litter.
instructions (n pl)★★★	/ɪnˈstrʌkʃənz/	Anweisungen	Listen carefully to the safety **instructions**.
intercontinental (adj)	/ˌɪntəkɒntɪˈnentəl/	Auslands-; interkontinental	For **intercontinental** flights, check in two hours before take-off.
packet (n)★	/ˈpækɪt/	Paket	Never offer to take a **packet** onto a plane for someone else.
paint (v)★★	/peɪnt/	malen	Do you enjoy **painting** pictures?
permission (n)★★	/pəˈmɪʃən/	Erlaubnis	Competitors under 16 must have their parents' **permission**.

priority (n)★★	/praɪˈɒrɪti/	Priorität	Safety and security are the top **priority** for all airlines.
safety (n)★★★	/ˈseɪfti/	Sicherheit	The **safety** of our passengers is a top priority.
scissors (n pl)	/ˈsɪzəz/	Schere	You mustn't have sharp things like knives or **scissors** in your hand baggage.
security (n)★★★	/sɪˈkjʊərɪti/	Sicherheitsmaßnahmen	**Security** at airports is a top priority nowadays.
sharp (adj)★★★	/ʃɑːp/	scharf	You're not allowed to carry **sharp** objects like knives or scissors.
sign (v)★	/saɪn/	unterschreiben	You must **sign** your entry form yourself.
take exercise	/ˌteɪk ˈeksəsaɪz/	sich Bewegung verschaffen	It's important to eat well and **take exercise** regularly.
warm up	/wɔːm ˈʌp/	aufwärmen	If you **warm up** snow you get water.
X-ray (n)	/ˈeks reɪ/	Röntgenaufnahme	Baggage **X-rays** at airports can take a long time.

GRAMMAR SUMMARY

Present simple (Einfaches Präsens): *be*
Unit 1 THIS IS YTV

Aussage

Vollform	Kurzform	Frage
I am	I'm	am I?
you are	you're	are you?
he is	he's	is he?
she is	she's	is she?
it is	it's	is it?
we are	we're	are we?
you are	you're	are you?
they are	they're	are they?

Negativform

Vollform	Kurzform
I am not	I'm not
you are not	you aren't
he is not	he isn't
she is not	she isn't
it is not	it isn't
we are not	we aren't
you are not	you aren't
they are not	they aren't

- In Fragen mit dem Verb *be* steht die Verbform immer vor dem Subjekt:
  Are you English?
  Where is Pedro from?
- Die Negativform wird durch Hinzufügen von *not* gebildet.
- Wir verwenden die Vollform in positiven und die Kurzform in negativen Kurzantworten:
  Yes, she is. No, she isn't.

Present simple (Einfaches Präsens)
Unit 1 Lessons 1 and 3

Aussage	Negativform Vollform	Kurzform
I like	I do not like	I don't like
you like	you do not like	you don't like
he likes	he does not like	he doesn't like
she likes	she does not like	she doesn't like
it likes	it does not like	it doesn't like
we like	we do not like	we don't like
you like	you do not like	you don't like
they like	they do not like	they don't like

Frageform	Kurzantworten	
Do you like...?	Yes, I do.	No, I don't.
	Yes, we do.	No, we don't.
Does he like...?	Yes, he does.	No, he doesn't.
Does she like...?	Yes, she does.	No, she doesn't.
Does it like...?	Yes, it does.	No, it doesn't.
Do they like...?	Yes, they do.	No, they don't.

- Wir verwenden das *present simple*, um Zustände, Routinen, Stundenpläne und regelmäßige Handlungen zu beschreiben:
  I go to the movies on Saturdays.
  She loves pigeons.
  Carol speaks Italian.
  What languages do you speak?
  Do you really speak Chinese?
  I don't play on my computer.
  She doesn't speak Chinese.

- Wir verwenden das *present simple*, um über Tätigkeiten im Berufsleben zu sprechen:
  What do you do? (= *What's your job?*)
  I'm a TV producer.
  I make sure that the film is good.

- In Aussagesätzen mit dem *present simple* ändert sich die Verbform nicht – außer nach *he, she, it*:
  he lives she lives it lives

- *Present simple* Negativform: Subjekt + *do/does not* + Verb:
  He doesn't play on his computer.

- *Present simple* Frageform: *do/does* + Subjekt + Verb.
  In Fragen mit *does* endet das Hauptverb nicht mit einem *s*:
  Does she likes̷ computers?

53

Present continuous (Verlaufsform des Präsens)
Unit 1 Lessons 2 and 3, Unit 5 Lesson 1

Aussagesätze

Vollform	Kurzform
I am talking	I'm talking
you are talking	you're talking
he is talking	he's talking
she is talking	she's talking
it is talking	it's talking
we are talking	we're talking
you are talking	you're talking
they are talking	they're talking

Negativsätze

I am not talking	I'm not talking
you are not talking	you aren't/you're not talking
he is not talking	he isn't/he's not talking
she is not talking	she isn't/she's not talking
it is not talking	it isn't/it's not talking
we are not talking	we aren't/we're not talking
you are not talking	you aren't/you're not talking
they are not talking	they aren't/they're not talking

Frageform	Kurzanworten
Are you talking?	Yes, I am.
	No, I'm not.
	Yes, we are.
	No, we aren't. No, we're not.
Is he/she/it talking?	Yes, he/she/it is.
	No, he/she/it isn't.
	No, he's/she's/it's not.
Are they talking?	Yes, they are.
	No, they aren't. No, they're not.

- Wir verwenden das *present continuous*, um über Ereignisse von kurzer Dauer zu sprechen und zu beschreiben, was gerade in diesem Augeblick geschieht:
  You're standing on my foot.
  He's wearing a YTV badge.
  They're holding hands.
  What are they doing?
  Is he helping her?
  He isn't helping her.
  They aren't holding hands.

- Wir können das *present continuous* auch verwenden. um über Pläne und Vereinbarungen für die Zukunft zu sprechen. Dabei nennen wir oft den Zeitpunkt und/oder den Ort:
  Greg is taking people to the Science Museum.
  We're returning to the hotel at 5.30pm.
  They aren't having lunch at the hotel.
  What time are they having lunch?
  Who is taking them to the Science Museum?
  How long are they spending at the museums?

- Schreibweise: Verb + *-ing*
  Bei den meisten Verben wird *–ing* hinzugefügt:
  stand – standing hold – holding

  Bei Verben, die mit -e enden, wird das -e gestrichen und dann erst *–ing* hinzugefügt:
  take – taking leave – leaving

  Other verbs:
  swim – swimming run – running
  put – putting sit – sitting

Possessive adjectives and Possessive pronouns (Possessivpronomen)
Unit 1 Lesson 3

Possessive adjectives		Possessive pronouns	
my	our	mine	ours
your	your	yours	yours
his/her	their	his/hers	theirs

- *Possessive adjectives* ändern sich nicht in Verbindung mit Pluralformen:
  my book my books

- Vor *possessive pronouns* wird kein *the* verwendet:
  This book is the mine.

- Um nach dem Besitzer von etwas zu fragen, verwenden wir das Fragewort *Whose*:
  Whose are the glasses?
  Whose is this book? OR Whose book is this?

Possessive forms: 's and s' (Possessivformen/Genitiv mit Apostroph und s)
Unit 1 Lesson 3

- Im Singular wird dem Substantiv ein 's (Apostroph s) hinzugefügt:
  the producer's job   Kate's boots

- Im Plural wird nur ein ' (Apostroph) hinzugefügt. Das Substantiv endet mit s' (Apostroph s):
  the actors' coffee break   the girls' bags

- Bei unregelmäßigen Pluralformen wird (wie im Singular) ein 's hinzugefügt:
  people's pockets   the women's bags

Comparative and superlative adjectives (Steigerung der Adjektive: Komparativ und Superlativ)
Unit 2 Lesson 1

Adjektiv	Komparativ	Superlativ
einsilbige		
small	smaller	the smallest
large	larger	the largest

einsilbige mit einfachem Vokal + einfachem Konsonanten am Ende:

big	bigger	the biggest
hot	hotter	the hottest

zweisilbige mit –y am Ende

noisy	noisier	the noisiest
silly	sillier	the silliest

mehrsilbige

famous	more famous	the most famous
exciting	more exciting	the most exciting

Unregelmäßige Formen

good	better	the best
bad	worse	the worst

- Bei einigen zweisilbigen Adjektiven wird -er/est oder -r/st hinzugefügt:

clever	cleverer	the cleverest
simple	simpler	simplest

- Das Gegenteil von *more* ist *less*:
  It's less expensive than Rio!

- Das Gegenteil von *most* ist *least*:
  They stayed in the least expensive hotel.

should/shouldn't
Unit 2 Lesson 2

- Wir verwenden *should* und *shouldn't (should not)*, um Ratschläge zu erteilen:
  We should stay together.
  You should tell me where you're going.
  You shouldn't go off on your own.
  Why should they tell Greg?

- *should* ist ein modales Hilfsverb:
  – es ändert sich nicht mit *he/she/it*.
  – es gibt kein *to* zwischen *should* und dem Hauptverb:
  You should ~~to~~ take flowers.

Prepositions of place (Präpositionen des Ortes)
Unit 2 Lesson 2

over   under   in front of   behind   between
inside   outside   next to   near   opposite

- *in front of* ist das Gegenteil von *behind*:
  Ben can't see because Carol is in front of him.

- *opposite* bedeutet "gegenüber":
  Page 21 is opposite page 20.

The gerund (-ing form) – (Das Gerundium)
Unit 2 Lesson 3

- Das Gerundium ist ein Substantiv, das von einem Verb abgeleitet wird. Es wird nach folgenden Verben verwendet:
  like, love, hate, enjoy, und *can't stand*:
  I love going to festivals.
  I hate being lost.
  I don't enjoy being rude.
  I can't stand waiting for people.
  What do you like doing?

- Das Gerundium wird auch nach Präpositionen verwendet:
  You're good at dancing.
  I'm not interested in listening to bossy people.

Past simple (Einfache Vergangenheit)

Unit 3 Lessons 1 and 2

be

Aussage	Negativform
I/he/she/it was	I/he/she/it wasn't (was not)
we/you/they were	we/you/they weren't (were not)

Frageform	Kurzantworten
Were you ...?	Yes, I was.
	No, I wasn't.
	Yes, we were.
	No, we weren't.
Was he/she/it ...?	Yes, he/she/it was.
	No, he/she/it wasn't.
Were they ...?	Yes, they were.
	No, they weren't.

- Von *be* gibt es nur zwei Formen der einfachen Vergangenheit:
  Everything was very dry.
  The people were asleep.
  The fire wasn't near his house.
  There weren't many buildings left.

- In der Frageform steht das Subjekt immer nach dem Verb *was/were*:
  Was Jack asleep all morning?
  Were they exhausted?

Regelmäßige Verben

Aussage		Negativform	
I		I	
you		you	
he/she/it	started	he/she/it	didn't start
we		we	(did not start)
you		you	
they		they	

Frageform	Kurzantworten
Did you start?	Yes, I/we did.
	No, I/we didn't. (did not)
Did he/she/it start?	Yes, he/she/it did.
	No, he/she/it didn't. (did not)
Did they start?	Yes, they did.
	No, they didn't. (did not)

- Schreibweise:
  Aussageform bei regelmäßigen Verben
  Bei den meisten Verben wird –*ed* hinzugefügt:
  start – started destroy – destroyed
  Bei Verben, die bereits mit -*e* enden, wird *d* hinzugefügt:
  escape –escaped die –died
  Bei Verben, die mit einem Konsonanten und -*y* enden, wird das -*y* gestrichen und –*ied* hinzugefügt:
  carry – carried marry – married

- *Past simple* Negativform: Subjekt + *didn't* + Verb:
  The fire didn't cross the river.

- *Past simple* Frageform: *did* + Subjekt + Verb:
  What did you do?
  How/When did they cross the river?
  Did you have fun?
  Did they see a play?

Unregelmäßige Verben

- Eine vollständige Liste aller in Inspiration 2 verwendeten Unregelmäßigen Verben finden Sie auf Seite 127.

- Unregelmäßige Verben bilden ihre Negativ- und Frageformen genau so wie regelmäßige Verben:
  They didn't have time to take a lot with them.

Adverbial phrases of time (Adverbien der Zeit)

Unit 3 Lesson 2

- Bei Wochentagen und Datumsangaben verwenden wir *on*:
  on Saturday (morning) on 21 August

- Bei Zeitabschnitten während des Tages, bei Monaten und Jahreszahlen verwenden wir *in*:
  in the morning in August in 1666

- Für ganz spezifische Zeitpunkte verwenden wir *at*:
  at 9am at noon/midnight

  und in einigen Redewendungen:
  at night at the weekend

Past continuous (Verlaufsform der Vergangenheit)
Unit 3 Lesson 3

Aussage
I/he/she/it was listening
we/you/they were listening

Negativform
I/he/she/it wasn't listening
we/you/they weren't listening

Frageform
Were you listening?

Kurzantworten
Yes, I was.
No, I wasn't.
Yes, we were.
No, we weren't.

Was he/she/it listening?
Yes, he/she/it was.
No, he/she/it wasn't.

Were they listening?
Yes, they were.
No, they weren't.

- Die Verlaufsform der Vergangenheit verwenden wir, um zu beschreiben, was gerade während einer bestimmten Zeit in der Vergangenheit passierte, um den Hintergrund eines Ereignisses darzustellen:

    At 2.30pm we were passing the London Eye.

- Wir bilden das *past continuous* mit *was/were* + *-ing* form:
    I was listening to Greg
    I wasn't looking   when Ben fell in.
    She was taking photos   at 2.30pm.
    We were passing the London Eye

    What was he doing? What were you doing?
    Was he feeling all right?

Why ...? because (reason) – (Begründung)
Unit 3 Lesson 3

- Wir verwenden das Bindewort *because*, um die Frage *Why...?* zu beantworten:
    Why did Sally shout 'Help!'?
    She shouted 'Help!' because Ben fell overboard.

going to (Futur mit going to)
Unit 4 Lesson 1

Aussage
I'm
you're
he's
she's   going to
it's
we're
they're

Negativform
I'm not
you aren't/you're not
he isn't/he's not
she isn't/she's not   going to
it isn't/it's not
we aren't/we're not
they aren't/they're not

Frageform
Are you going to?

Kurzantworten
Yes, I am. Yes, we are.
No, I'm not. No, we aren't.
No, we're not.

Is he/she/it going to?
Yes, he/she/it is.
No, he/she/it isn't.
No, he's/she's/it's not.

Are they going to?
Yes, they are.
No, they aren't. No, they're not.

- Wir verwenden *going to* + Infinitiv, um über feste Absichten und Pläne für die Zukunft zu sprechen:
    I'm going to take you on a tour of the studio.
    I'm not going to tell you now.
    Are we going to be here all day?
    What are you going to do?

- Wir verwenden *going to* + Infinitiv auch, um etwas für die Zukunft vorauszusagen, wenn wir in der gegenwärtigen Situation sehen können, dass es wahrscheinlich passieren wird:
    They're going to start the rehearsal.

Future simple: will/won't (Einfaches Futur mit will/won't)
Unit 4 Lesson 2

- Wir verwenden *will* und *won't* (will not), um Hoffnungen für die Zukunft auszudrücken oder ganz allgemeine Voraussagen zu machen:
    I'll miss working with Liam.
    We'll see each other again.
    I won't have anyone to talk to.
    What will Simon do with the gun?
    Will Robbie escape?

- *will* ist ein modales Hilfsverb:
  - Es ändert sich nicht mit *he/she/it*.
    I think he will escape.
    He won't be in Westsiders after this week's episode.

  - Es gibt kein *to* zwischen *will* und dem Hauptverb.
    I hope he'll to keep in touch.

Adverbs of manner (Adverbien der Art und Weise)
Unit 4 Lesson 3

Regelmäßigr		**Unregelmäßig**	
Adjektiv	Adverb	Adjektiv	Adverb
bad	badly	early	early
normal	normally	fast	fast
proper	properly	good	well
quick	quickly	hard	hard
proper	properly	late	late
quick	quickly		
comfortable	comfortably		
angry	angrily		
happy	happily		

- Adverbien beschreiben die Art und Weise, wie etwas gemacht wird:
    You spoke too fast.
    Actors work really hard.

- Schreibweise:
    Bei den meisten Adjektiven wird *–ly* hinzugefügt:
    normal – normally proper – properly

    Bei Adjektiven, die mit einem *-y* enden, wird das *y* gestrichen und *–ily* hinzugefügt:
    happy – happily angry – angrily

    Bei Adjektiven, die mit *-ble* enden, wird das *-e* gestrichen und *–y* hinzugefügt:
    comfortable – comfortably terrible – terribly

Sequencing adverbs (Adverbien der Zeitenfolge)
Unit 5 Lesson 1

First they're visiting London Zoo.
Next they're walking along the Regent's Canal.
Then they're having lunch.
After that, they're going shopping.
Finally they're taking a canal boat trip.

- Wir verwenden diese Adverbien, um eine Zeitenfolge bei bestimmten Ereignissen zu beschreiben. Die Adverbien *next, then,* und *after that* können in jeder beliebigen Reihenfolge verwendet werden.
- Nach *after that* folgt immer ein Komma.

Object pronouns (Personalpronomen als (Akkusativ)Objekt)
Unit 5 Lesson 2

Singular	Plural
me	us
you	you
him, her, it	them

- Diese Form der Personalpronomen verwenden wir nach Verben und Präpositionen:
    I can show him the way.
    Can you help us?
    Listen to me.
    I'm waiting for him.

Verb + indirect and direct object (Verben mit indirektem und direktem Objekt)
Unit 5 Lesson 2

- Viele Verben können zwei Objekte haben:
    I'll give you a map.
    (you = indirektes Objekt; a map = direktes Objekt)
    I'll ask her the way.
    (her = indirektes Objekt; the way = direktes Objekt)

- Folgende Verben können indirekte und direkte Objekte haben:
    ask bring buy give send sing take write

- Das indirekte Objekt mit einer Präposition kann nach dem direkten Objekt stehen:
    She bought a present for him.
    I'll give the map to you.

Prepositions of direction (Präpositionen der Richtungsangabe)
Unit 5 Lesson 2

across   along   up   down   past
round   through   to   into

- Folgende Beispiele mit *across* und *through* sollte man sich merken::

  across { the bridge / the river / the street / the room / the road }

  through { the trees / the crowd / the door / the window / the rain }

- Wir verwenden *down* und manchmal *up* mit der gleichen Bedeutung wie *along* – auch wenn es überhaupt keinen Hang gibt!
  We ran down the road to the bus stop.
  He walked up the path to the front door.

some and *any*
Unit 5 Lesson 3

- Wir verwenden *some* und *any* mit Pluralformen und mit unzählbaren Substantiven.
- Wir verwenden *some* in positiven Aussagesätzen und in Bitten und Fragen, wenn die Antwort, die wir erwarten oder wollen, „Ja" ist:
  I'd like some garlic bread.
  Could I borrow some money?

- Wir verwenden *any* in negativen Sätzen und in neutralen Fragen:
  I don't want any olives/meat.
  Have you got any pizzas with mushrooms?

How much/many? (Wie viel/Wie viele?)
Unit 5 Lesson 3

- Wir verwenden *How much . . .?* mit unzählbaren Substantiven:
  How much money have you got?
  How much bread do you want?

- Wir verwenden *How many . . .?* mit Pluralformen und zählbaren Substantiven:
  How many colas?
  How many people are there?

Countable and uncountable nouns (Zählbare und unzählbare Substantiven)
Unit 5 Lesson 3

- Zählbare Substantive haben eine Singular- und eine Pluralform:
  a tomato – tomatoes   an olive – olives

- Mit unzählbaren Substantiven wird kein *a/an* verwendet:
  We like cheese.   Do you want some bread?

- Unzählbare Substantive stehen immer nur im Singular:
  It's rice.   Spaghetti comes from Italy.

Present perfect (vollendete Gegenwart)
Unit 6 Lessons 1 and 2

Aussage
I/you/we/they have worked
he/she/it has worked

Kurzform
I/you/we/they've worked
he/she/it's worked

Negativform
I/you/we/they have not worked
he/she/it has not worked

I/you/we/they haven't worked
he/she/it hasn't worked

Frageform
Have you worked?

Has he/she/it worked?

Have they worked?

Kurzantworten
Yes, I/we have.
No, I/we haven't.

Yes, he/she/it has.
No she/he/it hasn't.

Yes, they have.
No, they haven't.

- Wir können das *present perfect* verwenden, um über Handlungen oder Ereignisse zu sprechen, die gerade oder vor kurzem zu Ende gingen bzw. abgeschlossen wurden.
  I have tried to talk to her.
  She has been horrible to me.
  Have you recorded anything?
  Yes, I have.
  Have you had an argument with her?
  No, I haven't.
  What has Carol recorded?

Dabei wird die genaue Zeit der Handlung oder des Ereignisses nicht erwähnt. Wir können aber auf einen längeren, bis jetzt noch nicht zu Ende gegangenen Zeitabschnitt hinweisen:
all day, today, this week/month/year.
She hasn't said a word to me all day.
Have you had fun this week?

- Wir können das *present perfect* mit *just* verwenden, um über Ereignisse die sprechen, die gerade passiert sind:
  I've just worked out how to use the camera.
  I've just filmed you two.

- Wir können das *present perfect* auch verwenden, oft mit *ever/never*, um über persönliche Erfahrungen aus einer unbestimmten Zeit in der Vergangenheit zu sprechen.
  - *ever* = jemals. Es wird hauptsächlich in Fragen verwendet:
  Have you ever felt really stupid?
  Have you ever had a girlfriend?

- *ever* wird auch in positiven Aussagesätzen nach Superlativen verwendet:
  It's the best film I've ever seen.

- *never* = (noch) nie/niemals:
  I've never been so embarrassed.
  She has never seen anyone so angry before.

- Das *present perfect* wird mit *have/has* + *past participle* gebildet.

- Bei regelmäßigen Verben hat das *past participle* die gleiche Form wie das *past tense* (einfache Vergangenheit): work, worked, worked

- Bei einigen unregelmäßigen Verben hat das *past participle* die gleiche Form wie das *past tense*, aber bei vielen ist die Form völlig anders: be, was/were, been.

Eine vollständige Liste aller in Inspiration 2 verwendeten Unregelmäßigen Verben finden Sie auf Seite 127.

- Das *past participle* von *go* kann entweder *gone* oder auch *been (= gone and returned)* sein:
  He's gone to Rio. = He's in Rio now.
  He's been to Rio. = He's visited Rio but he's not there now.

too much/too many and *(not) enough* (zu viel/zu viele und (nicht) genug)
Unit 6 Lesson 3

- *too much* wird mit unzählbaren Substantiven verwendet:
  They cost too much money.
  Don't make too much noise.

- *too many* wird mit den Pluralformen von zählbaren Substantiven verwendet:
  There are too many tourists.
  There are too many queues.

- *enough* steht immer vor einem Substantiv:
  There isn't enough time.
  aber nach Adjektiven und Adverbien:
  Is that loud enough?

must and *mustn't* (müssen und nicht dürfen)
Unit 7 Lesson 1

- Wir verwenden *must*, um eine Verpflichtung in der Gegenwart oder Zukunft auszudrücken – oft in Verbindung mit einer Regel oder Vorschrift:
  The celebrities must give up luxuries.
  They must learn survival techniques.
  What kind of things must they do?

- Wir verwenden die Negativform *mustn't (must not)* dagegen, um ein Verbot auszudrücken:
  They mustn't take mobile phones.
  They mustn't forget the dangers of the jungle.

- *must* ist ein modales Hilfsverb:
  – Es ändert sich nicht mit *he/she/it.*
  – Es gibt kein *to* zwischen *must* und dem Hauptverb.
  They must to eat insects and worms.

- Das *past tense* (einfache Vergangenheit) von *must* ist *had to*:
  One person had to walk through water full of crocodiles.

- *must* ist starker als *should*.

have/has to and *don't/doesn't have to* (müssen und nicht müssen)
Unit 7 Lesson 2

- Wir können auch *have/has to*, um eine Verpflichtung in der Gegenwart oder Zukunft auszudrücken:
  I have to do some shopping.
  Carol has to buy some presents.
  Do we have to go?

- Wir verwenden *don't/doesn't have to*, wenn eine Verpflichtung nicht besteht:
  You don't have to come with me.

- Sowohl *have to* als auch *must* können in der Aussageform verwendet werden, um eine Verpflichtung auszudrücken. Aber:
  don't/doesn't have to = Es ist nicht notwendig.
  mustn't = Es ist nicht erlaubt.

- Das *past tense* von *must* und *have to* ist in beiden Fällen *had to*:
  We had to stay there for ages.

Participial adjectives ending in -ed/-ing (Partizipien als Adjektive)
Unit 7 Lesson 3

- Adjektive, die mit -ed enden, beschreiben ein Gefühl oder eine Reaktion:
  You'll be surprised by the human body.
  Don't be frightened!

- Adjektive, die mit -ing enden, beschreiben die Ursache für das Gefühl oder die Reaktion:
  There are lots of surprising fish.
  Earthquakes are shocking.

- Die folgenden *participial adjectives* kommen sehr oft vor:
  amazed – amazing   bored – boring   excited – exciting
  fascinated – fascinating   frightened – frightening
  interested – interesting   shocked – shocking
  surprised – surprising   tired – tiring

Infinitive of purpose (Infinitivform – Absicht)
Unit 8 Lesson 1

- Wir verwenden die Infinitivform mit *to* (*infinitive of purpose*), um zu erklären, warum wir etwas tun:
  They use models to make the films.
  Nick Park joined the studio to work on a film.
  The animator uses the storyboard to plan the film.

Verb + infinitive (Verben + Infinitivform)
Unit 8 Lesson 1

- Wir verwendene *to* + Infinitiv nach bestimmten Verben:
  The BBC offered to buy one of their first films.
  They decided to call it Aardman.
  They often only manage to make three seconds of film.

- Wir können *to* + Infinitiv auch nach diesen Verben und Redewendungen verwenden:
  agree ask decide know how learn manage
  mean need offer pretend promise refuse
  seem teach tell want would like

Open conditional with *if/when* (Einfache Bedingungssätze)
Unit 8 Lesson 2

- Wir verwenden Bedingungs- oder Konditionalsätze, um über Ursache und Wirkung zu sprechen:
  If you like a boy, you're rude.
  When I'm on my own, I get depressed.
  When we mix red and green, we get yellow.

- In offenen oder einfachen Bedingungsaätzen, stehen beide Verben im einfachen Präsens (*present simple tense*).

- Der Nebensatz mit *if/when* kann auch nach dem Hauptsatz stehen:
  I don't like it when people tell me what to do.
  What do you do if people are bossy?
  How do you feel when you're on your own?

ALPHABETICAL INDEX

A

a bit (adv) p.25
a third (n) p.34
abbreviation (abbrev) (n) p.33
absolutely (adv) p.45
absorb (v) p.33
absurd (adj) p.27
accept p.30
accident (n) p.29
across (prep) p.31
act (v) p.25
acting company (n) p.22
action (n) p.25
action-packed (adj) p.29
activity (n) p.27
actor (n) p.4
actually (adv) p.35
add (v) p.51
addictive (adj) p.35
address (n) p.13
adjective (n) p.29
adult (n) p.47
adverb (n) p.29
advertisement (n) p.45
advice (n) p.33
aerobics (n) p.2
afraid (adj) p.26
after (prep) p.18
again (adv) p.6
ages (n pl) p.42
agree (with) (v) p.13
air travel (n) p.51
airport (n) p.39
alive (adj) p.43
All right. p.7

all-night (adj) p.11
alone (adv) p.40
along (prep) p.31
also (adv) p.8
alternative (n) p.33
amazed (adj) p.43
amazing (adj) p.11, p.43
American (adj) p.1
amongst (prep) p.43
amphibian (n) p.43
angel (n) p.39
angrily (adv) p.28
angry (adj) p.6
animal (n) p.36
animated display (n) p.43
animation (n) p.48
animator (n) p.48
annoyed (adj) p.38
annoying (adj) p.33
answer (n) p.1
answer (v) p.13
anyone (pron) p.26
anything (pron) p.17
anywhere (adv) p.35
apartment (n) (AmE) p.24
appear (v) p.25
aquarium (n) p.8
architect (n) p.20
area (n) p.24
argue (v) p.48
arrangement (n) p.31
arrival (n) p.16
arrive (v) p.13
artificial (adj) p.33
ask (v) p.13

asleep (adj) p.18
at first p.21
at home p.7
at the end of p.11
at the moment p.7
audience (n) p.40
Australia (n) p.1
autograph (n) p.40
auxiliary verb (aux) p.33
(on) average p.51
award (n) p.40

B

baby (n) p.43
background (n) p.48
backpack (n) p.33
backpacker (n) p.33
backpacking (n) p.33
backwards (adv) p.29
bacon (n) p.47
bad at p.15
badge (n) p.3
badly (adv) p.28
bag (n) p.3
baggage (n) p.51
baker's (n) p.18
ball (n) p.11
balloon (n) p.38
ball-point pen (n) p.18
band (n) p.11
bangle (n) p.4
bank (n) p.13
bar (n) p.45
baseball cap (n) p.6
basic (adj) p.40

bathroom (n) p.46
be born (v) p.18
beach (n) p.16
beans (n pl) p.40
bear (n) p.36
beautiful (adj) p.22
beautifully (adv) p.30
become (v) p.18
bed (n) p.2
bedroom (n) p.45
before (prep) p.6
behind (prep) p.13
behind (prep) p.3
bell (n) p.8
bend (v) p.47
Best wishes (as formula for ending letter) p.25
bestseller (n) p.22
between (prep) p.13, p.20
bicycle (n) p.21
big (adj) p.8
big wheel (n) p.8, p.21
billion p.40
bird (n) p.2, p.36
birthday (n) p.7
biscuit (n) (BrE) p.24
bite (n) p.40
blow (v) p.48
boat (n) p.8
body language (n) p.47
bone (n) p.50
bonfire (n) p.18
book (n) p.6
book (v) p.13
bookshop (n) p.13
border (n) p.39
boring (adj) p.25
borrow (v) p.32

boss (n) p.5
bossily (adv) p.28
bossy (adj) p.15
bow (v) p.47
box of matches (n) p.40
boy (n) p.1
boyfriend (n) p.6
brain (n) p.43
brandy (n) p.18
Brazil (n) p.1
bread (n) p.13, p.32
break (v) p.36
breakfast (n) p.2
bridge (n) p.19
briefcase (n) p.5
brightness (n) p.49
brilliant (adj) p.20
bring (v) p.16
bring to life p.50
broadcast (n) p.28
broadcast (v) p.28
build (v) p.19
building (n) p.19
burn (v) p.16
burn down (phr v) p.20
bury (v) p.19
bus (n) p.21
bus driver (n) p.38
bus station (n) p.38
bus stop (n) p.38
bus ticket (n) p.38
bus timetable (n) p.38
busker (n) p.3
busy (adj) p.30
butter (n) p.19
button (n) p.49
buy (v) p.7

by (prep) p.19
Bye! (interj) p.13

C
calculation (n) p.49
call (= name someone/something) (v) p.1
call (= telephone) (v) p.1
camera (n) p.3
cameraman (n) p.5
camp (n) p.40
camp (v) p.25
camping site (n) p.25
can't stand p.16
canal (n) p.8
candle (n) p.16, p.40
capsule (n) p.8
car (n) p.21
car crash (n) p.5
car driver (n) p.38
car engine (n) p.38
car park (n) (BrE) p.24
car park (n) p.38
caravan park (n) p.29
cardboard box (n) p.33
care (v) p.42
career (n) p.23
careful (adj) p.8
carefully (adv) p.29
carnival (n) p.11
carriage (n) p.18
carry (v) p.13
cartoon (n) p.26
cassette (n) p.24
cassette recorder (n) p.24
cast (n) p.25
cat (n) p.26
catch (a train/bus) (v) p.42

cathedral (n) p.8
CD player (n) p.50
celebrate (v) p.11
celebration (n) p.16
celebrity (n) p.40
cell phone (n) (AmE) p.24
central (adj) p.18
centre (n) p.8
century (n) p.19
certainly (adv) p.32
chair (n) p.25
champagne (n) p.16
change some money p.13
channel (n) p.38
character (n) p.28
charity (n) p.40
chat (v) p.2
chat show (n) p.26
cheap (adj) p.25
cheaply (adv) p.33
cheat (v) p.51
check (n) p.51
check-out (n) p.42
cheek (n) p.13
cheer up (phr v) p.38
cheese (n) p.19
cheese (n) p.32
chemist's (n) p.13
children (n pl) p.13
chips (n pl) (BrE) p.24
choose (v) p.11
chopping board (n) p.41
Christmas Day (n) p.9
Christmas tree (n) p.18
church (n) p.9
cinema (n) p.2
city (n) p.9

clap (v) p.41
clean (v) p.43
clearly (adv) p.43
climb (v) p.9
clock (n) p.9
clock tower (n) p.9
close (adj) p.19
close (v) p.30
closed (adj) p.35
cloth (n) p.33
clothes (n pl) p.6
coast (n) p.23
coffee (n) p.5
coffee break (n) p.5
cold (adj) p.11
collect (v) p.23
colour (n) p.6
colour (v) p.50
colourful (adj) p.11
column (n) p.9
come (v) p.5
come back (phr v) p.13
come down (phr v) p.20
Come on! p.31
comfortable (adj) p.28
comfortably (adv) p.28
comment (n) p.47
commercial (n) p.31
common (adj) p.47
communicate (v) p.47
compare (v) p.49
competition (n) p.1
competitor (n) p.51
complain (v) p.41
complete (adj) p.20
computer (n) p.2
computer chip (n) p.49

computer expert (n) p.48
contact (n) p.41
contact (v) p.50
contestant (n) p.41
continue (v) p.7
conversation (n) p.36
cook (v) p.41
cooking pot (n) p.41
cool (adj) p.35
copy (v) p.29
corner (n) p.31
correct (adj) p.2
cosmopolitan (adj) p.11
cost (v) p.17
costume (n) p.11
cotton (n) p.33
countable (C) p.33
country (n) p.11
cover (v) p.47
covered with p.24
cow (n) p.36
crazy (adj) p.26
create (v) p.39
creature (n) p.44
crocodile (n) p.41
cross (v) p.19
cross-country skiing (n) p.45
crowd (n) p.13
crowded (adj) p.33
cruise (n) p.21
cry (v) p.21
culture (n) p.45
cup (of coffee/tea) (n) p.13
curtains (n pl) p.26
customer (n) p.32
cycle (v) p.6

D

dairy produce (n) p.32
dance (v) p.15
dancer (n) p.11
danger (n) p.41
dangerous (adj) p.5
date (n) p.47
daypack (n) p.33
death (n) p.23
decide (v) p.23
deep (adj) p.44
deer (n) p.36
definitely (adv) p.35
department store (n) p.31
depressed (adj) p.49
describe (v) p.19
design (v) p.19
designer (n) p.48
designer clothes (n pl) p.35
destroy (v) p.19
details (n pl) p.43
develop (v) p.44
diary (n) p.19
dictionary (n) p.6
die (v) p.19
diet (n) p.35
different (adj) p.2
difficult (adj) p.6
digital photo (n) p.50
dinner (n) p.8
dinosaur (n) p.44
direction (n) p.13
director (n) p.5
disagree (v) p.47
disco (n) p.35
discover (v) p.24
do the ironing p.43
do the shopping p.43
do the washing up p.43
doctor (n) p.29
documentary (n) p.26
dog (n) p.6
double-decker bus (n) p.9
down (adj) p.50
down (prep) p.35
dragon (n) p.16
drama (n) p.26
drama exercise (n) p.28
drink (v) p.2, p.16
drive (v) p.38
drugstore (n) (AmE) p.24
drum (n) p.26
drummer (n) p.11
dry (adj) p.11
dry (v) p.33
duck (n) p.37
during (prep) p.41
Dutch (adj) p.24
DVD player (n) p.50

E

early (adv) p.13, p.28
earthquake (n) p.44
easily (adv) p.29
Easter (n) p.18
easy (adj) p.6
eat (v) p.2, p.13
electric (adj) p.38
email (n) p.37
embarrassed (adj) p.38
emergency (n) p.29
emergency number (n) p.21
empty (adj) p.38
encourage (v)
English (adj) p.1
enjoy (v) p.15
enjoyable (adj) p.51
enough (adj) p.18
enter (a competition) (v) p.43
entry form (n) p.51
envelope (n) p.16
environment (n) p.44
episode (n) p.28
equal to p.9
equipment (n) p.41
erupt (v) p.44
eruption (n) p.44
escape (v) p.19
evening (n) p.2
event (n) p.19
every (adj) p.2
everyone (pron) p.3
everything (pron) p.13
exact (adj) p.9
exactly (adv) p.9
exam (n) p.36
excited (adj) p.44
exciting (adj) p.9
Excuse me. p.5
exhausted (adj) p.20
exhausting (adj) p.45
exhibition (n) p.20
exist (v) p.50
exotic (adj) p.11
expensive (adj) p.5
experience (v) p.44
experienced (adj) p.33
explain (v) p.30
explorer (n) p.24
extinct (adj) p.44
extra (adj) p.32

extraordinary (adj) p.44
extremely (adv) p.23
eye (n) p.19

F
face to face p.9
facial expression (n)
fact (n) p.20
factory (n) p.23
failure (n) p.18
fall (v) p.21
fame (n) p.23
famous (adj) p.9
fantastic (adj) p.15
far (adj) p.31
farm (n) p.37
fascinated (adj) p.44
fascinating (adj) p.44
fast (adv) p.28
fast-moving (adj) p.29
fatal (adj) p.51
favourite (adj) p.6
feather (n) p.44
feed (v) p.44
feel (v) p.21
feeling (n) p.50
ferry boat (n) p.39
festival (n) p.11
field (n) p.19
fight (n) p.5
film (n) p.2
film (v) p.30
film character (n) p.9
film crew (n) p.41
film star (n) p.9
film-maker (n) p.49
filter (n) p.50

finally (adv) p.23
finally (adv) p.6
find (v) p.13
find out (phr v) p.6
fire (n) p.9
fireworks (n pl) p.16
fish (n) p.2
fit (adj) p.51
flame (n) p.19
flash (v) p.45
flash photograph (n) p.41
flat (BrE) (n) p.24
fleece (n) p.3
flight (n) p.13
flower (n) p.3
flower shop (n) p.13
follow (v) p.11
food (n) p.8
football (n) p.2
for (prep) p.19
for short p.1
foreign (adj) p.11
forest (n) p.24
forget (v) p.18
fork (n) p.35
fortnight (n) p.41
fortunately (adv) p.41
fortune (n) p.23
fortune teller (n) p.50
free (adj) p.27
freezing (adj) p.45
French fries (n pl) (AmE) p.24
fried egg (n) p.32
friend (n) p.1
friendly (adj) p.37
frightened (adj) p.44
frightening (adj) p.44

from (prep) p.1
frown (n) p.46
fruit (n) p.9
full of p.11
fun (n) p.9
funny (adj) p.21

G
game (n) p.16
game show (n) p.27
garbage (n) (AmE) p.24
garlic (n) p.32
garlic bread (n) p.32
gerund (n) p.29
gesture (n) p.47
get (v) p.13
get on (well) (phr v) p.27
get up (phr v) p.17
ghost story (n) p.23
giant (adj) p.11
giraffe (n) p.37
girl (n) p.3
girlfriend (n) p.6
give up (phr v) p.41
glass (n) p.32
glasses (n pl) p.5
go away (phr v) p.14
go back (to) (phr v) p.37
goat (n) p.37
good (adj) p.2
good at p.15
good luck p.16
Goodbye! p.8
graded reader (n) p.50
grammar (n) p.24
grape (n) p.16
grass (n) p.38

great (adj) p.5
greetings card (n) p.16
ground (n) p.51
group (n) p.3
grow (v) p.44
guess (v) p.6
guest (n) p.14
guidebook (n) p.38
guitar (n)
gun (n) p.26
guy (n) p.36
guys (form of address) (n pl) p.20

H
haircut (n) p.14
hairdresser's (n) p.14
half an hour p.7
halfway (adv) p.39
ham (n) p.32
happen (v) p.3
happily (adv) p.28
happy (adj) p.7
harbour (n) p.24
hard (adj) p.39
hard (adv) p.28
hat (n) p.3
hate (v) p.15
have a go p.27
have a great time p.5
have a shower (n) p.37
have an argument p.26
have fun p.20
hear of (phr v) p.39
heavy (adj) p.33
heavy metal (n) p.15
helicopter (n) p.21
help (v) p.3

herd (n) p.45
herd (v) p.45
Hey! (interj) p.5
hidden camera (n) p.41
hide (v) p.41
high (adj) p.9
highlight (n) p.44
Hindu (adj) p.18
Hindu (n) p.18
hippo (n) p.37
history (n) p.9
hit (n) p.40
hit (v) p.22
hold hands p.3
holiday (n) p.1
homework (n) p.17
honestly (adv) p.32
hope (v) p.5
hopeless (adj) p.32
horrible (adj) p.37
horse (n) p.37
hospital (n) p.29
hot (adj) p.19
house (n) p.15, p.16
household name (n) p.40
How about ...? p.2
How long? p.11
How many? p.12
hug (v) p.47
huge (adj) p.35
human being (n) p.44
hungrily (adv) p.29
hungry (adj) p.12
Hurry up! p.31
hurt (v) p.20
husky (dog) (n) p.45

I
I'm afraid (= I'm sorry) p.27
I've no idea. p.22
ice (n) p.45
ice cream (n) p.20
illness (n) p.29
image (n) p.50
imaginary (adj) p.29
immediately (adv) p.14
important (adj) p.7
impossible (adj) p.24
in (prep) p.19
in charge of p.5
in contrast p.47
in detail p.49
in fact p.9
in front of (prep) p.13
in the middle of p.37
including (prep) p.12
increased (adj) p.45
infinitive (n) p.29
inflammable (adj) p.19
information (n) p.50
inhabitant (n) p.45
insect (n) p.41
inside (prep) p.14
instead (adv) p.33
instructions (n pl) p.51
intelligent (adj) p.44
interact (v) p.44
interactive (adj) p.44
intercontinental (adj) p.51
interest (n) p.47
interested (in) (adj) p.15
interesting (adj) p.9
into (prep) p.31
invent (v) p.19

inventor (n) p.49
invite (v) p.47
island (n) p.25
It depends. p.6
item (n) p.41

J

jacket (n) p.3
jazz (n)Which p.15
jeans (n pl) p.3
jewellery (n) p.14
job (n) p.5
join (v) p.23
joke (n) p.2
joke (v) p.37
journalist (n) p.49
judge (n) p.12
jump (v) p.14
jungle (n) p.41

K

keep in touch p.27
keep warm p.33
kid (n) p.36
kill (v) p.26
kind p.12
king (n) p.9
kiss (v) p.14
kitchen (n) p.46
knife (n) p.35
know (v) p.2

L

language (n) p.2
Lapland (n) p.45
large (adj) p.12
last (v) p.12
late (adv) p.2

late (adv) p.28
later (adv) p.20
laugh (v) p.22
lay eggs p.44
lay the table p.43
lazy (adj) p.20
learn (v) p.7
leave (v) p.8
left (adj) p.5
left (adv) p.31
lentils (n pl) p.16
Let me see. p.3
library (n) p.46
lifebelt (n) p.22
lift (n) p.18, p.39
light (v) p.16
lights (n pl) p.5
lightweight (adj) p.33
like (v) p.2
lion (n) p.16, p.37
listen (to) (v) p.3
litter (n) p.41
live (adj) p.41
live (v) p.7
loads of ... p.36
local (adj) p.29
log (n) p.41
log fire (n) p.41
long (adj) p.12
look (at) (v) p.2
look after (phr v) p.14
look down p.9
look forward to (phr v) p.7
look out p.9
lose (v) p.15
lost (adj) p.14
lots of p.9

loud (adj) p.12
loudly (adv) p.28
love (v) p.2, p.15
luckily (adv) p.19
lunch (n) p.20
luxury (n) p.41

M

madam (form of address) (n) p.35
magazine (n) p.14
magazine (n) p.5
major (adj) p.23, p.45
make a film p.5
make a noise p.39
make a wish p.17
make sure that p.5
make your bed p.43
make-up (n) p.41
mammal (n) p.44
man (pl men) (n) p.3
manage to do sth p.49
manager (n) p.27
map (n) p.4
market (n) p.9
marriage (n) p.36
marry (v) p.19
match (n) p.42
material (n) p.33
mathematics (n) p.50
meal (n) p.14
mean (= intend) (v) p.50
mean (v) p.4
means of transport (n) p.46
meanwhile (adv) p.48
measure (v) p.50
meat (n) p.32
medicine (n) p.14

meet (v) p.5
melt (v) p.46
member (n) p.17
menu (n) p.35
microphone (n) p.26
millimetre (mm) (n) p.49
mind (n) p.44
mirror (n) p.42
miss (= not see) (v) p.31
miss (v) p.7, p.9
mistake (n) p.7
mix (v) p.50
mobile (phone) (n) p.18
model (n) p.36
model (n) p.49
model (n) p.9
money (n) p.12
monkey (n) p.37
monument (n) p.9
moon (n) p.50
mountain (n) p.39
move (to) (v) p.23
move (v) p.8
move over (phr v) p.26
murderer (n) p.29
museum (n) p.10
mushroom (n) p.32
music programme (n) p.27
musical (n) p.38
musician (n) p.39, p.49

N
Native American (n) p.25
near (prep) p.14
need (v) p.28
nervous (adj) p.28
nervously (adv) p.28
new (adj) p.10

New Year p.17
New Year's Eve p.17
(bad) news (n) p.28
news programme (n) p.27
newsagent's (n) p.14
newspaper (n) p.23
next (adj) p.23
next to (prep) p.14
next to p.4
nice (adj) p.12
nightclothes (n pl) p.19
No entry p.42
No way! p.46
noisy (adj) p.12
nonsense (n) p.25
non-stop (adj) p.12
noodles (n pl) p.17
normally (adv) p.28
not ... until (prep) p.21
notebook (n) p.5
nothing (pron) p.7
notice (v) p.15
noun (n) p.29
novel (n) p.23
novelist (n) p.23
nurse (n) p.29

O
obsessive (adj) p.36
of course (not) p.2
offer (v) p.49
office (n) p.46
oil (n) p.19
old (adj) p.12
olive (n) p.32
on (prep) p.20
on fire p.19
on time p.43

on your own p.14
once (adv) p.14
onion (n) p.32
online (adv) p.2
open (adj) p.10
open (v) p.14
open space (n) p.37
opposite (prep) p.14
order (v) p.32
ordinary (adj) p.33
organise (v) p.36
original (adj) p.46
ourselves (pron) p.28
outside (prep) p.14
outside world (n) p.42
over (prep) p.14
overboard (adv) p.22
Ow! (interj) p.21
own (adj) p.10

P
pack (v) p.20
packet (n) p.51
paint (v) p.51
painting (n) p.40
pants (n pl) (AmE) p.25
parade (n) p.12
parade (v) p.12
paraffin (n) p.42
Pardon? p.8
park (n) p.7
parking lot (n) (AmE) p.25
part-owner (n) p.23
party (n) p.17
pass (an exam) (v) p.43
pass (v) p.22
passenger p.8
passport (n) p.40

past (prep) p.10, p.31
patient (n) p.30
payment (n) p.21
pepper (n) p.32
percentage (n) p.36
perfect (adj) p.31
perform (v) p.17
performance (n) p.21, p.28
performer (n) p.30
permission (n) p.51
phone (v) p.2
phone call (n) p.20
phone card (n) p.18
pickpocket (n) p.5
picnic lunch (n) p.21
piece (n) p.25
pig (n) p.37
pigeon (n) p.2
pillar (n) p.39
pilot (n) p.49
pineapple (n) p.32
pixel (n) p.50
place (n) p.10
plan (n) p.26
plan (v) p.49
plane (n) p.22
planet (n) p.37
plate (n) p.14
play (a part/role) (v) p.5
play (n) p.23
play (the guitar/piano etc) p.7
play (v) p.2
playwright (n) p.23
pleased (adj) p.27
plural (pl) (adj) p.34
pocket (n) p.5
poem (n) p.17

point (n) p.3
point (v) p.22
poisonous (adj) p.42
Poland (n) p.1
police officer (n) p.31
police station (n) p.14
politely (adv) p.28
polyester (n) p.34
pool (n) p.27
pop (n) p.15
popular (adj) p.10
population (n) p.1
position (n) p.48
post office (n) p.14
power (n) p.44
practise (v) p.28
prefer (v) p.27
preposition (n) p.30
present (adj) p.21
present (n) p.14
presenter (n) p.1
press (v) p.50
primary colour (n) p.50
print (v) p.20
priority (n) p.52
prison (n) p.27
prize (n) p.1
probably (adv) p.23
problem (n) p.5
process (n) p.49
producer (n) p.5
promise (v) p.30
pronoun (n) p.30
properly (adv) p.28
protect (v) p.37
provide (v) p.44
pub (n) p.30

publish (v) p.23
pull (v) p.22
pull someone's leg p.37
pullover (n) p.4
punk (n) p.15
purse (n) p.4
put (v) p.4
put away (phr v) p.43

Q
queen (n) p.10
questionnaire (n) p.14
queue (n) p.39
Quick! (interj) p.4
quickly (adv) p.28
quiet (adj) p.12
quietly (adv) p.28

R
railroad (n) (AmE) p.25
railway (n) (BrE) p.25
railway engine (n) p.38
railway line (n) p.38
railway station (n) p.38
rain (n) p.20
rain (v) p.22
raincoat (n) p.34
rainforest (n) p.44
raise (money) (v) p.46
rap (n) p.15
rather (I'd rather ...) p.45
reach (v) p.20
read (v) p.7
ready (adj) p.30
real (adj) p.10
realise (v) p.34
reality TV show (n) p.42

reason (n) p.39
rebuild (v) p.10
receive (v) p.21
recent (adj) p.30
record (n) p.10
record (v) p.24
record shop (n) p.21
recording (n) p.26
referee (n) p.49
refuse (v) p.49
reggae (n) p.12
region (n) p.12
rehearsal (n) p.26
rehearse (v) p.26
reindeer (n) p.46
relationship (n) p.27
relax (v) p.7
replica (n) p.46
reptile (n) p.45
rescue (v) p.22
respond (v) p.48
responsibility (n) p.36
return (v) p.20
revenge (n) p.27
revise (v) p.51
rhino (rhinocerous) (n) p.42
rice (n) p.17
rich (adj) p.23
ride (n) p.10
ride (v) p.10
right (adv) p.31
right-hand (adj) p.39
ring (v) p.17
river (n) p.1
roar (v) p.46
robbery (n) p.30
rock (n) p.16, p.22

rocket (n) p.22
romance (n) p.30
rope (n) p.27
round (prep) p.31
rucksack (n) p.34
rude (to) (adj) p.16
rudely (adv) p.28
run (v) p.4

S
sad (adj) p.28
sadly (adv) p.28
safe (adj) p.14
safety (n) p.52
sail (v) p.22
salt (n) p.10
same (adj) p.15
satellite TV (n) p.39
save (v) p.49
say (v) p.12
scan (v) p.51
scarf (n) p.6
school (n) p.23
schoolboy (n) p.49
scissors (n pl) p.52
screen (n) p.51
scriptwriter (n) p.6
sea monster (n) p.3
seat (n) p.8
seat belt (n) p.43
seawater (n) p.10
security (n) p.52
see (v) p.4
sell (v) p.8
send (v) p.17
sentence (n) p.43
serious (adj) p.30

set (v) p.51
setting (n) p.30
several (adj) p.23
shake hands p.15
shampoo (n) p.42
shark (n) p.10
sharp (adj) p.52
sheep (n) p.37
shine (v) p.22
ship (n) p.3
shirt (n) p.4
shiver (v) p.22
shocking (adj) p.45
shoe (n) p.4
shoot (a film) (v) p.6
shoot (v) p.26
shopping (n) p.10
short (adj) p.7
shorts (n pl) p.7
should (v) p.15
shoulder (n) p.34
shout (v) p.50
show (n) p.12
show (v) p.18
side (n) p.39
sight (n) p.39
sightseeing (n) p.4
sign (n) p.15
sign (v) p.52
silence (n) p.26
simulator (n) p.38
sing (v) p.18
singer (n) p.30
single (n) p.40
singular (sing) (adj) p.34
sir (form of address) p.8
sit (v) p.8

site (n) p.10
sitting room (n) p.47
size (n) p.12
skin (n) p.34
skirt (n) p.6
sky (n) p.10
sled (n) p.46
slow (adj) p.10
slowly (adv) p.29
small (adj) p.12
smart (adj) p.12
smile (v) p.22
smoke (n) p.20
smoke (v) p.42
snake (n) p.42
sneakers (n pl) (AmE) p.25
snow (n) p.46
snowmobile (n) p.46
soap (opera) (n) p.26
somebody (sb) p.34
someone (pron) p.7
something (sth) p.34
soon (adv) p.23
soul (n) p.16
sound (n) p.37
sound system (n) p.12
soup (n) p.17, p.35
space (n) p.20
spaceship (n) p.22
Spain (n) p.1
Spanish (adj) p.1
speak (v) p.3
special (adj) p.7
special effects (n pl) p.43
species (n) p.37
spectacular (adj) p.12
speedboat (n) p.22

spell (v) p.3
spend (money) (v) p.36
spend (time) (v) p.21
spider (n) p.35
spinach (n) p.32
splash (v) p.51
spoon (n) p.42
sports programme (n) p.27
spring (n) p.46
square (n) p.50
squirrel (n) p.37
stage (n) p.12
stall (n) p.12
stamp (n) p.15
stand (v) p.21
stand (v) p.4
stare (v) p.48
start (n) p.17
start (v) p.10
starving (I'm ...) (adj) p.32
station (n) p.8
statue (n) p.39
stay (v) p.7
stay silent (adj) p.48
steak (n) p.35
steal (v) p.4
steep (adj) p.39
step (n) p.21
stone (n) p.10
stop (v) p.4
store (n) (AmE) p.25
storm (n) p.22
story (n) p.23
storyboard (n) p.49
stranger (n) p.18
strap (n) p.34
street (n) p.12

street party (n) p.12
street theatre (n) p.10
stretch (v) p.46
strong (adj) p.34
student (n) p.26
studio (n) p.26
study (v) p.20
stuff (n) p.34
stunning (adj) p.46
stuntman/stuntwoman (n) p.6
stupid (adj) p.16
success (n) p.23
suddenly (adv) p.22
sugar (n) p.6
suggest (v) p.34
suggestion (n) p.34
suit (n) p.34
suitcase (n) p.17, p.34
summer (n) p.7
sunglasses (n pl) p.6
sunshine (n) p.7
superior (n) p.48
supermarket (n) p.15
supplies (n pl) p.42
surf (v) p.26
surf the Internet p.21
surprise (n) p.26
surprising (adj) p.45
survey (n) p.36
survival technique (n) p.42
sweater (n) p.34
sweatshirt (n) p.4
swim (v) p.26
swimming (n) p.3
swimming pool (n) p.47
swimming trunks (n pl) p.34

Swiss (adj) p.1
Switzerland (n) p.1

T

table (n) p.32
table manners (n pl) p.48
take (v) p.4
take a picture (of) p.22
take exercise p.52
take off (phr v) p.48
take part p.42
take photographs p.4
take place p.30
take-off (n) p.43
talk (about) (v) p.4
tall (adj) p.10
task (n) p.42
tea (n) p.3
teach (v) p.3
teacher (n) p.7, p.23
techno (n) p.16
teenager (n) p.36
tell (v) p.4
temper (n) p.50
temple (n) p.39
terribly (adv) p.27
terrific (adj) p.22
test (v) p.45
text message (n) p.49
Thank goodness! (interj) p.22
thank you p.15
thatched roof (n) p.21
the Dutch (n) p.24
the future (n) p.26
the law (n) p.43
the left (n) p.31
the movies p.2

the rest (of you) (n) p.14
the right (n) p.31
the top (of) (n) p.21
the whole of ... p.39
theft (n) p.27
then (adv) p.20
thing (n) p.3
think (v) p.7
thirstily (adv) p.30
thirsty (adj) p.21
thoughtfully (adv) p.48
thrill (n) p.45
thriller (n) p.27
through (prep) p.32
throw (v) p.17
ticket (n) p.8
tie (n) p.34
tie up (phr v) p.27
tiger (n) p.37
time difference (n) p.30
tiny (adj) p.50.
tip (= suggestion) (n) p.34
tired (adj) p.21
tiring (adj) p.45
to (prep) p.32
together (adv) p.15
toilet paper (n) p.42
tomato (n) p.32
top (n) p.4
tortoise (n) p.45
total (adj) p.36
touch (v) p.42
tour (n) p.10
tour guide (n) p.4
tourism (n) p.46
tourist (n) p.6
tourist attraction (n) p.10

tourist centre (n) p.46
tourist guide (n) p.49
tradition (n) p.17
traditional (adj) p.17
traditionally (adv) p.46
traffic (n) p.38
tragedy (n) p.23
train (n) p.8
train driver (n) p.38
train station (n) p.38
train ticket (n) p.38
train timetable (n) p.38
trainer (n) p.4
trash (n) (AmE) p.25
travel (v) p.10
travel agency (n) p.15
travel sack (n) p.34
travel writer (n) p.34
traveller (n) p.34
treat (n) p.26
treat (v) p.36
treatment (n) p.42
trip (n) p.31
trouble (n) p.30
trousers (n pl) p.4
trust (n) p.48
trust (v) p.36
truth (n) p.7
try (v) p.7
T-shirt (n) p.4
tube (n) p.38
tundra (n) p.46
turn left/right p.32
turn round (phr v) p.34
TV programme (n) p.8
twice (adv) p.15
typewriter (n) p.24

U

umbrella (n) p.4
uncountable (U) (adj) p.35
under (prep) p.15
underground (n) p.31
understand (v) p.30
underwear (n) p.17
unfriendly (adj) p.48
unhappy (adj) p.36
until (prep) p.23
unusual (adj) p.10
up (prep) p.32
upset (adj) p.36
use (v) p.16

V

valuable (adj) p.27
vegetable (n) p.10
vegetarian (adj) p.32
verb (n) p.30
version (n) p.46
video recorder (n) p.51
view (n) p.10
viewer (n) p.42
village (n) p.30
visit (n) p.42
visit (v) p.4
vocabulary (n) p.25
volcano (n) p.45

W

wait (for) (v) p.15
waiter (n) p.8
walk (n) p.27
walk (v) p.15
Walkman (n) p.20
want (v) p.8

warm (adj) p.12
warm up p.52
wash (v) p.35
watch (n) p.6
watch (v) p.3, p.4
water (n) p.17
water cycle (n) p.45
waterfalls (n pl) p.39
waterproof (adj) p.35
wave (n) p.17
wave about (v) p.35
wear (v) p.4
weather (n) p.12
website (n) p.8
wedding (n) p.46
week (n) p.1
weigh (v) p.10
weight (n) p.10
well (adj) p.26
well (adv) p.29
well-known (adj) p.13
well-known (adj) p.24
Western (adj) p.48
wet (adj) p.13
whale (n) p.22
What a shame! p.28
What on earth ...? p.22
when (adv) p.24
whisper (v) p.11
whistle (n) p.49
whistle (v) p.22
wild (adj) p.37
wildlife (n) p.37
win (v) p.1
wind (n) p.20
window (n) p.17
windy (adj) p.46

wine (n) p.17
wine (n) p.20
winner (n) p.1
wool (n) p.35
word (n) p.7
work (n) p.21
work (v) p.24
work out (phr v) p.31, p.37
world (n) p.11, p.16
world-famous (adj) p.39
worldwide (adj) p.40
worm (n) p.42
worried (adj) p.31, p.46
worry (v) p.26
write (v) p.6
writer (n) p.24
wrong (adj) p.35

X

X-ray (n) p.52

Y

You're right. p.5
young (adj) p.35

Z

zoo (n) p.11

Vocabulary Extra!

UNIT 1 Making friends

LESSON 1 Do you really speak Chinese?

1 Lies die Wörter und höre dir dann die Tonaufnahme an. Worüber reden die einzelnen Sprecher? Schreibe die Ziffern 1–11 in die richtigen Kästchen.

- a ☐ birds
- b ☐ breakfast
- c ☐ the cinema
- d ☐ a computer
- e ☐ 1 the evening
- f ☐ a film
- g ☐ fish
- h ☐ football
- i ☐ a joke
- j ☐ languages
- k ☐ tea

2 Lies die Wörter, dann höre dir die Tonaufnahme an. Welche sind die richtigen Satzendungen? Schreibe die Ziffern 1–9 in die richtigen Kästchen.

- a ☐ to the movies?
- b ☐ my breakfast.
- c ☐ French?
- d ☐ football?
- e ☐ any good jokes?
- f ☐ secondary school.
- g ☐ spell your name?
- h ☐ 1 tea or coffee at breakfast?
- i ☐ to her friends online.

LESSON 2 You're standing on my foot!

3 Höre dir die Tonaufnahme an und schreibe dann diese Namen unter die richtigen Bilder.

Amy   Laura   Megan   Nicole   Rachel   Sarah

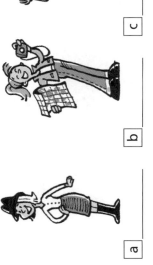

a _____   b _____   c _____

d _____   e _____   f _____

4 Höre dir die Tonaufnahme an und markiere das richtige Bild (✓)

1   a ☐   b ☐   c ☐

2   a ☐   b ☐   c ☐

3   a ☐   b ☐   c ☐

4   a ☐   b ☐   c ☐

5   a ☐   b ☐   c ☐

LESSON 3   What's the producer's job?

5 Höre dir die Tonaufnahme an und ordne die Berufe den richtigen Personen zu.

Personen		Berufe
1 ☐ Ryan	a	actor
2 ☐ Josie	b	cameraman
3 ☐ Ross	c	director
4 ☐ Chris	d	scriptwriter
5 ☐ Chloe	e	stuntman

6 Höre dir die Tonaufnahme an. Welches Wort steht am Ende der einzelnen Sätze? Schreibe die Ziffern 1–7 in die richtigen Kästchen.

a ☐ expensive
b ☐ glasses
c ☐ magazine
d ☐ pocket
e ☐ scarf
f ☐ sugar
g ☐ tourists

LESSON 4   Personal profiles

7 Lies die Antworten, dann ordne die Fragen, die du in der Tonaufnahme hörst, diesen Antworten zu. Schreibe die Ziffern 1–6 in die richtigen Kästchen.

Antworten

a ☐ It depends.
b ☐ I'm a film producer.
c ☐ Let me see them, please!
d ☐ Of course not. It's a joke, silly!
e ☐ What do you mean?
f ☐ You're right! Sorry!

PRONUNCIATION

Welche Silbe wird betont – die erste oder die zweite? Schreibe die Wörter in die entsprechende Spalte. Überprüfe deine Antworten, indem du die Tonaufnahme anhörst.

Br~~azil~~   language   breakfast   correct
behind   problem   again   relax   goodbye
sunshine   happen

■■	■■
tourist	_Brazil_

CULTURE   Welcome to London

Wo befinden sich die Sprecher oder was schauen sie sich an? Höre dir die Tonaufnahme an und schreibe die Ziffern 1–8 in die richtigen Kästchen.

a ☐ an aquarium
b ☐ a canal
c ☐ a church
d ☐ a city
e ☐ a clock
f ☐ a double-decker bus
g ☐ a market
h ☐ 1 a taxi

77

UNIT 2 Festivals

LESSON 1 Europe's best street party

1 Höre dir die Tonaufnahme an. Welches Wort steht am Ende der einzelnen Sätze? Schreibe die Ziffern 1–9 in die richtigen Kästchen.

a ☐ cold
b ☐ colourful
c ☐ hungry
d ☐ large
e [1] loud
f ☐ quiet
g ☐ real
h ☐ smart
i ☐ well-known

2 Ergänze die Sätze mit dem richtigen Wort. Überprüfe deine Antworten, indem du dir die Tonaufnahme anhörst.

| carnival   country   judge   parade   reggae |
| stall   stage |

1 _____ is a kind of music.
2 Brazil is a _____ which I'd like to visit.
3 People wear costumes and dance in the streets during _____.
4 That's the _____. She chooses the best dancers and gives them a prize.
5 The band is on the _____ now. They're getting ready to play.
6 The dancers _____ in the streets for two days. They all wear amazing costumes.
7 We usually buy our fruit at that _____ in the market.

LESSON 2 We should stay together

3 Höre dir die Tonaufnahme an und schreibe die Namen in das Bild.

Andy   Carol   Dave   Liam   Maria   Sam

78

4 Lies die Antworten, dann ordne die Sätze, die du in der Tonaufnahme hörst, diesen Antworten zu. Schreibe die Ziffern 1–7 in die richtigen Kästchen.

Antworten

a ☐ At the supermarket.
b ☐ Is he booking our flights to Spain?
c ☐ No, but there's a bank in King Street.
d ☐ OK. Do you want me to buy some medicine for you?
e ☐ The same as you probably! I'm buying stamps.
f ☐ There's a good hairdresser's opposite the bank.
g ☐ Yes, I want to get a music magazine.

LESSON 3 I love going to festivals

5 Höre dir die Tonaufnahme an und ordne die Sätze 1–6 den Beschreibungen a–f zu.

a ☐ She's bossy.
b ☐ She's good at it.
c ☐ She hates it.
d ☐ She's interested in it.
e ☐ She loves it.
f ☐ She's rude.

LESSON 4 Celebrations

6 Worüber reden die einzelnen Sprecher? Höre dir die Tonaufnahme an und schreibe die Ziffern 1–9 in die richtigen Kästchen.

a ☐ the beach
b ☐ candles
c ☐ champagne
d ☐ an envelope
e ☐ fireworks
f ☐ games
g ☐ rice
h ☐ a suitcase
i ☐ windows

7 Lies die Antworten und ordne dann die Sätze, die du hörst, den richtigen Antworten zu. Schreibe die Ziffern 1–6 in die richtigen Kästchen.

Antworten

a ☐ No! Why should I?
b ☐ Oh, I don't know.
c ☐ Please don't. I want to be on my own.
d ☐ Music, dancing, Japanese food.
e ☐ Really? Why not?
f ☐ Yes, you do! You have lots.

PRONUNCIATION

1 Höre genau zu und streiche die stummen Buchstaben in diesen Wörtern durch.

country   weather   well-known   bread
flight   should   techno   foreign   champagne
interested   jewellery   sign

2 Höre zu und markiere die Silbe, die betont wird.

ad<u>dress</u>   carnival   celebration
exotic   fantastic   festival
hairdresser   immediately   magazine
medicine   parade   questionnaire
spectacular   supermarket   traditional

UNIT 3 Past times

LESSON 1 The fire started at the baker's

1 Höre dir die Tonaufnahme zweimal an. Du hörst die Lebensgeschichte von Theobold Chuzzlewit. Du wirst bestimmt nicht jedes Wort verstehen, aber das macht nichts. Versuche beim zweiten Mal die Sätze den Bildern zuzuordnen.

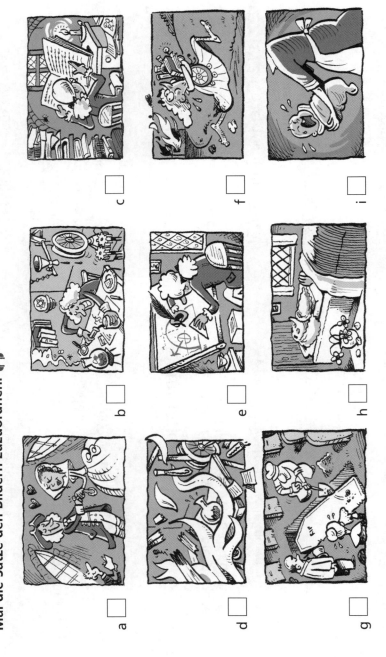

a ☐   b ☐   c ☐
d ☐   e ☐   f ☐
g ☐   h ☐   i ☐

LESSON 2 Did you have fun?

2 Bringe die Buchstaben der Wörter in Klammern in die richtige Reihenfolge. Schreibe dann die richtigen Wörter in die Lücken. Überprüfe deine Antworten, indem du dir die Tonaufnahme anhörst.

1 I eat _____ (cie-marce) a lot in the summer.
2 That _____ (carichett) designed the fantastic building opposite our house.
3 The _____ (crefnoperam) was fantastic. The dancers were brilliant.
4 There were two hundred and fifty _____ (pests). We were very tired when we got to the top.
5 My father says he doesn't like _____ (krow) but he spends a lot of time doing it.
6 The CDs in that _____ (corder hops) were very expensive. I didn't buy anything.
7 There are some great black and white photos of New York at the _____ (hibexoniti).
8 For our _____ (cincip) on the beach, we had cheese sandwiches and chocolate cake.

3 Lies die Fragen. Höre dir die Tonaufnahme an und ordne die verschiedenen Sprecher diesen Fragen zu. Schreibe die jeweilige Ziffer in das entsprechende Kästchen.

a ☐ Who is exhausted?
b ☐ Who knows lots of facts?
c ☐ Who is having fun?
d ☐ Who is lazy?
e [1] Who is thirsty?
f ☐ Who is surfing the Internet?
g ☐ Who is standing at the top of a high building?
h ☐ Who spent the day sightseeing?

LESSON 3 What was he doing?

4 Worüber reden die einzelnen Sprecher? Höre zu und schreibe die Ziffern 1–7 in die richtigen Kästchen.

- a ☐ bicycle
- b ☐ car
- c ☐ bus
- d ☐ plane
- e ☐ helicopter
- f ☐ spaceship
- g ☐ 1 speedboat

5 Ergänze die Sätze mit dem richtigen Wort. Überprüfe deine Antworten, indem du dir die Tonaufnahme anhörst.

> crying feeling laughing ~~passing~~ sailing shining shivering smiling

1 Can I come in for five minutes? I was just _passing_.
2 Are you OK? How are you _____?
3 I took a picture of her but she didn't look good. She wasn't _____.
4 It was a beautiful hot day. The sun was _____.
5 It was really cold. I didn't have my jacket and I was _____.
6 It's not funny. Why are you _____?
7 The little girl was lost and she was _____.
8 They have a little boat and they love going _____.

LESSON 4 Biography

6 Ordne die Wortendungen den entsprechenden Wortanfängen zu. Überprüfe deine Antworten, indem du dir die Tonaufnahme anhörst.

1 GHOST _STORY_   PAPER
2 FACT _____   HER
3 BEST _____   ORY
4 NEWS _____   DY
5 NO _____   SELLER
6 PLAY _____   ~~STORY~~
7 TEAC _____   VEL
8 TRAGE _____   WRIGHT

7 Wer oder was wird in den folgenden Sätzen beschrieben? Schreibe das ganze Wort (aus Übung 6) in die dafür vorgesehene Lücke.

1 She works at Highgate School. She loves her students. A _____
2 You can read it in less than an hour. It's about a girl called Catherine. She dies in a fire. But after her death, people still see her at night. A _ghost story_
3 At the end of the play everyone dies. A _____
4 All my friends bought this book. It's the most popular book this year. A _____
5 He wrote a good one called *The Canal*. I saw it in a theatre in Liverpool last year. A _____
6 I buy the same one every day. It costs sixty pence and it's called *The Guardian*. A _____
7 It's by Henry James. It's good but the English is difficult. I didn't finish it. I reached page 345 and then I stopped. A _____
8 They make cars there. A _____

PRONUNCIATION

Höre zu und streiche die stummen Buchstaben in den einzelnen Wörtern durch.

> thatched whistle playwright ghost story whale factory building design cruise

CULTURE Hello New York!

Ordne die Wörter in amerikanischem Englisch, die du in der Tonaufnahme hörst, den Wörtern in britischem Englisch unten zu. Schreibe die Ziffern 1–8 in die richtigen Kästchen.

- a ☐ the chemist's
- b ☐ chips
- c ☐ 1 a car park
- d ☐ a film
- e ☐ a flat
- f ☐ the rubbish
- g ☐ a shop
- h ☐ trainers

81

UNIT 4 Soap

LESSON 1 Is he going to shoot someone?

1 Ordne die Wortendungen den entsprechenden Wortanfängen zu. Überprüfe deine Antworten, indem du dir die Tonaufnahme anhörst.

1 SOAP O_PERA_   AT
2 GU___   INS
3 MICRO___   IO
4 REHEA___   PERA
5 STUD___   PHONE
6 CURTA___   RSAL
7 DR___   UMS
8 FUT___   URE
9 TRE___

2 Worum handelt es sich? Schreibe das ganze Wort (aus Übung 1) in die dafür vorgesehene Lücke.

1 I always close them at night. I can't sleep with them open. _soap opera_
2 It's called *Southport Place*. It's on TV every evening at seven. A ___
3 Can you stand a bit closer to it? We can't hear you. A ___
4 Cathy plays them in a band. ___
5 The director wants all the actors to come to one tomorrow in Room 234. A ___
6 Put it down. You don't want to hurt anyone, do you? It's very dangerous. A ___
7 You can't go in there at the moment. They're filming. A ___
8 On Dad's birthday we had dinner in an expensive restaurant and then we all went to the theatre. It was great! A ___
9 I'm going to finish school and then I'd like to travel around the world. The ___

3 Jeder Sprecher spricht zwei Sätze. Höre dir den jeweiligen ersten Satz an, dann ordne ihn dem richtigen zweiten Satz unten zu. Schreibe die Ziffern 1–9 in die richtigen Kästchen.

Die zweiten Sätze

a ☐ I'm not going to watch another minute of it.
b ☐ It's near the sea.
c ☐ There are fifty actors.
d ☐ We can get cheap tickets.
e ☐ 7 Tonight we're going to find out who did it.
f ☐ First I'm going to go swimming with Alice. Then we're going to the cinema.
g ☐ That means they're doing a recording in Studio 3.
h ☐ Damien shot her because she was going out with another man.
i ☐ I'm taking you to New York next weekend.

LESSON 2 I'll miss him

4 Höre dir die Tonaufnahme an und ordne die Stimmen den verschiedenen Arten von Fernsehsendungen zu. Schreibe die Ziffern 1–7 in die richtigen Kästchen.

a ☐ cartoon
b ☐ 1 documentary
c ☐ game show
d ☐ music programme
e ☐ news
f ☐ sports programme
g ☐ thriller

5 Ergänze die Sätze mit dem richtigen Wort. Überprüfe deine Antworten, indem du dir die Tonaufnahme anhörst.

| argument manager pool pleased prison |
| revenge rope valuable ~~walk~~ |

1 Do you want to go shopping or shall we go for a _walk_ ?

2 He's quite bossy but that's because he's the ____.

3 I broke my brother's camera and he wasn't very ____.

4 I don't speak to her now. We had a terrible ____.

5 Let's go to the club and have a game of ____.

6 She has a lot of old stamps. Some of them are quite ____.

7 The police caught the thieves and they are now in ____.

8 Tony killed Mario's brother so Mario wanted ____.

9 I can't play the piano …. I can only play one thing.

8 She's going to buy an ____. It's ….

7 I bought tickets for the ____ P_RF_RM_NCE afternoon ….

6 I was late for school today, N_RM_LLY but I'm not ….

LESSON 3 You spoke too fast

6 Höre dir die Tonaufnahme an und ordne die Stimmen den entsprechenden Adverbien zu. Schreibe die Ziffern 1–8 in die richtigen Kästchen.

Wer sprach …

a ☐ angrily? f ☐ quickly?
b ☐ bossily? g ☐ quietly?
c [1] happily? h ☐ politely?
d ☐ loudly? i ☐ sadly?

7 Anhand der Hinweise versuche, die Wörter mit den fehlenden Vokalen zu vervollständigen. Überprüfe deine Antworten, indem du dir die Tonaufnahme anhörst.

1 We didn't buy this cake.
We made it …. OU_RSE_LVE_S

2 In this soap, Alan, the teacher, is my favourite …. CH_R_CT_R

3 I slept really well. My bed is really …. C_MF_RT_BL_

4 I'm going to work really … for the exams. H_RD

5 We're going to find out _P_S_D_ who killed him in the next ….

LESSON 4 TV programmes

8 Worüber reden die Sprecher? Höre dir die Tonaufnahme an und schreibe die Ziffern 1–7 in die richtigen Kästchen.

a ☐ a hospital
b ☐ a murderer
c ☐ a performer
d ☐ a pub
e ☐ a robbery
f ☐ a village
g [1] an illness

PRONUNCIATION

Höre genau zu und ordne diese Wörter entweder *drum* oder *shoot* zu.

~~cool~~ ~~come~~ fruit gun love Monday move pool pub rude through trouble who worry

/ʌ/ drum	/uː/ shoot
come	cool

83

UNIT 5 Out and about

LESSON 1 What's happening tomorrow?

1 Worüber reden die Sprecher? Höre dir die Tonaufnahme an und schreibe die Ziffern 1–8 in die richtigen Kästchen. 🎧

a ☐ arrangements
b ☐ a canal boat trip
c ☐ a commercial
d ☐ a museum
e ☐ a perfect holiday
f ☐ a theatre
g ☐ the underground
h ☐ 1 a zoo

LESSON 2 You can't miss it!

2 Höre dir die Tonaufnahme an und markiere das richtige Bild (✓). 🎧

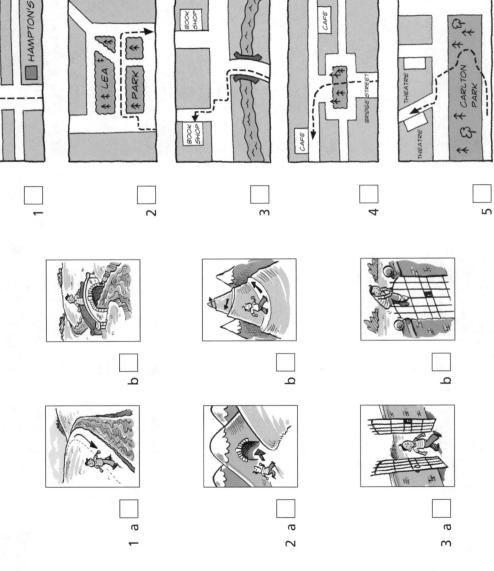

3 Höre dir die Wegbeschreibungen an. Passen die Angaben auf den unten stehenden Karten dazu (✓) oder nicht (✗)? 🎧

LESSON 3 Could I borrow some money?

4 Höre dir die Tonaufnahme an. Welches Wort passt zu den einzelnen Sätzen? Schreibe die Ziffern 1–8 in die richtigen Kästchen.

- a ☐ cheese
- b ☐ eggs
- c ☐ ham
- d [1] olives
- e ☐ onion
- f ☐ peppers
- g ☐ pineapple
- h ☐ spinach

LESSON 4 Suggestions and advice

5 Lies dir die Hinweise durch, dann schreibe die richtige Wörter. Überprüfe deine Antworten, indem du dir die Tonaufnahme anhörst.

1 A lot of men wear one to work. T _ie_____
2 It means 'full of people' C_____
3 It's warm. Sweaters are often made of it. W_____
4 Men wear them at the beach. S_____ T_____
5 You can wear one in bad weather to keep dry. R_____
6 The top part of your arms. S_____
7 T-shirts are usually made of it. C_____
8 When you buy a new TV or computer, it is usually in one of these. B_____
9 You put things in it when you go on holiday. S_____

6 Lies die Antworten. Ordne jeden Satz, den du in der Tonaufnahme hörst, diesen Antworten zu. Schreibe die Ziffern 1–8 in die richtigen Kästchen.

Antworten

- a ☐ Certainly, coming right up.
- b ☐ An orange juice, please.
- c [1] Certainly. What's the problem?
- d ☐ Go straight along this street. It isn't far. You can't miss it!
- e ☐ Honestly, you're hopeless!
- f ☐ We're all going to the beach for a picnic.
- g ☐ Would you like some chocolate?
- h ☐ Yes. Can I have a ham and olive pizza, please?

PRONUNCIATION

7 Welche Silbe wird betont – die erste oder die zweite? Schreibe diese Wörter in die richtige Spalte. Überprüfe deine Antworten, indem du dir die Tonaufnahme anhörst.

advice   along   annoy   backpack   disco   exam   extra   instead   menu   police   raincoat   shoulder   something   suggest   survey   upset

■ ■	■ ■
	advice

CULTURE Teenage life

8 Höre dir die Tonaufnahme an. Welche der drei Bedeutungen passt zu dem Satz, den du hörst?

1 a ☐ It's really helpful.
  b ☐ It's really bad.
  c ☐ It's a bit difficult to use.

2 a ☐ She went to work on a boat.
  b ☐ She went away to study.
  c ☐ She only ate certain things.

3 a ☐ She spends a lot of money on clothes.
  b ☐ She doesn't spend much on clothes.
  c ☐ Her parents pay for her clothes.

4 a ☐ It's boring.
  b ☐ You never want to stop playing it.
  c ☐ It's very slow.

5 a ☐ He is worried about Joss.
  b ☐ He is upset about Joss.
  c ☐ He is obsessive about Joss.

6 a ☐ He is unhappy about the future.
  b ☐ He doesn't have to think about money, work or the future.
  c ☐ Everyone treats him like a child.

85

UNIT 6 City life

LESSON 1 Have you recorded everything?

1 Höre dir die Sprecher in der Tonaufnahme an. Ordne die Tier-Wörter den entsprechenden Bildern zu. Schreibe die Ziffern 1–9 in die richtigen Kästchen.

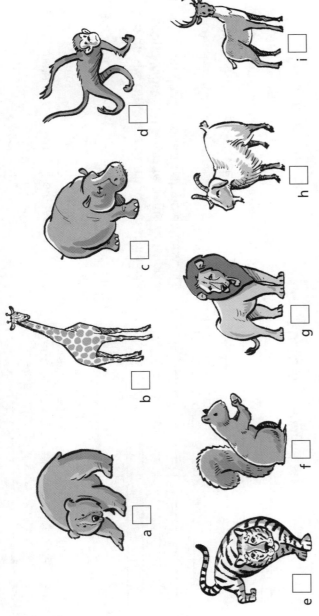

2 Höre dir die Tonaufnahme an. Über welche Tiere wird gesprochen? Schreibe die Ziffern 1–6 in die richtigen Kästchen.

a ☐ birds
b ☐ cows
c ☐ ducks
d ☐ horses
e ☐ pigs
f ☐ sheep

LESSON 2 Have you ever …?

3 Höre dir die Tonaufnahme an und ordne die Wörter, die du hörst, den Bildern zu. Schreibe die Ziffern 1–10 in die richtigen Kästchen.

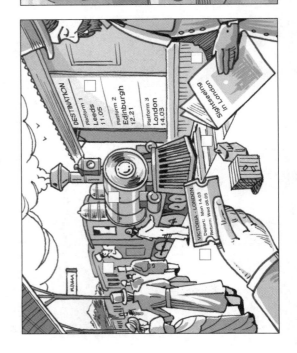

LESSON 3 Too many tourists

4 Höre zu und markiere (✓) das richtige Bild.

1 a ☐ b ☐
2 a ☐ b ☐
3 a ☐ b ☐
4 a ☐ b ☐
5 a ☐ b ☐
6 a ☐ b ☐
7 a ☐ b ☐

LESSON 4 Favourite places

5 Ordne die Wortendungen den entsprechenden Wortanfängen zu. Überprüfe deine Antworten, indem du dir die Tonaufnahme anhörst.

1 ANG *EL*   ALLS
2 BO _____   BOAT
3 FERRY _____ ~~EL~~
4 LI _____   FT
5 MOU _____   LAR
6 PIL _____   NTAIN
7 STAT _____ PLE
8 TEM _____   RDER
9 WATERF _____ UE

6 Lies die Antworten, dann ordne die Sätze, die du hörst, diesen Antworten zu. Schreibe die Ziffern 1–6 in die richtigen Kästchen.

Antworten

a ☐ Here she comes.
b ☐ I know but I'm really worried about Luisa.
c ☐ No, really, I'm not joking.
d ☐ OK. Let's go there then.
e ☐ *1* What's that?
f ☐ Why don't we ask your brother to help us?

PRONUNCIATION

Reimen sich diese Wortpaare? Markiere sie mit einem (✓) oder einem (✗). Überprüfe deine Antworten, indem du dir die Tonaufnahme anhörst.

1 bear   hear   ☐
2 bird   word   ☐
3 grass   has   ☐
4 horse   doors   ☐
5 joke   work   ☐
6 noise   boys   ☐
7 pull   wool   ☐
8 queue   view   ☐
9 shower flower ☐
10 sight   write   ☐
11 tiger   bigger ☐
12 wild   smiled ☐

UNIT 7 Wonderful world

LESSON 1 They must eat insects and worms

1 Höre dir die Tonaufnahme an. Ordne die Informationen den Bildern zu. Schreibe die Ziffern 1–7 in die richtigen Kästchen.

a ☐   b ☐
c ☐   d ☐
e ☐   f ☐
e ☐

2 Ordne die Wörter in Liste B den Wörtern in Liste A zu, um entsprechende Zusammensetzungen zu bilden. Überprüfe deine Antworten, indem du dir die Tonaufnahme anhörst.

Liste A	Liste B
1 chopping _board_	fire
2 cooking _____	board
3 film _____	crew
4 flash _____	paper
5 log _____	photograph
6 make- _____	pot
7 reality _____	technique
8 survival _____	TV
9 toilet _____	up

LESSON 2 Do we have to go?

3 Welche Art von Hilfe leisten diese Teenager zu Hause? Höre dir die Tonaufnahme an und schreibe die Namen in die entsprechende Lücke. Es gibt zwei Lücken mehr als notwendig.

| Ivan | Elly | Stuart | Josie | Dan | Alice | Sam |

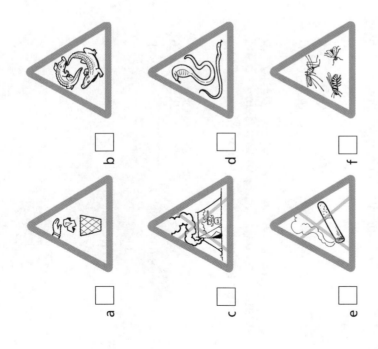

Ivan _____
_____
_____
_____
_____
_____
_____
_____

4 Höre dir die Tonaufnahme an. Worüber reden die Sprecher? Schreibe die Ziffern 1–6 in die richtigen Kästchen.

a ☐ a competition
b ☐ 1 a film
c ☐ a flight
d ☐ a law
e ☐ a supermarket
f ☐ an exam

LESSON 3 Don't be frightened!

5 Ordne die Antworten den richtigen Hinweisen zu. Überprüfe deine Antworten, indem du dir die Tonaufnahme anhörst.

Antworten

| amphibians | birds | dinosaurs | mammals |
| rainforest | reptiles | ~~volcano~~ | |

Hinweise

1 A mountain that sometimes erupts. _volcano_
2 Another word for *jungle*. _____
3 They feed their babies with milk. _____
4 Snakes and tortoises are in this group of animals. _____
5 They have feathers, lay eggs and can usually fly. _____
6 They can live in water and on land. _____
7 They're extinct now. _____

6 Was hielten diese Studenten von dem Museum? Höre dir die Tonaufnahme an und schreibe das richtige Wort in das entsprechende Kästchen.

frightening   boring   ~~shocking~~   surprising
fascinating   tiring

Mark	
Suzie	_shocking_
Liza	
Tom	
Maria	
Jack	

LESSON 4 Describing a journey

7 Lies die Antworten. Ordne jeden Satz, den du hörst, diesen Antworten zu. Schreibe die Ziffern 1–6 in die richtigen Kästchen.

Antworten

a ☐ Do you want to borrow a sweater?
b ☐ I don't care. I haven't got time to go to it.
c ☐ I'd rather have a horse!
d ☒ _1_ No way! I don't like the cold.
e ☐ Really? I think it sounds exciting.
f ☐ Yes! It's too good to miss.

PRONUNCIATION

Markiere in jedem Wort die Silbe, die betont wird. Überprüfe deine Antworten, indem du dir die Tonaufnahme anhörst.

ad**ver**tisement   equipment   poisonous
autograph   fortunately rainforest
contestant   luxury   shampoo
crocodile   meanwhile   thoughtfully

CULTURE Do the right thing!

Lies diese Wörter. Dann höre dir die Tonaufnahme an. Welches Wort passt zu welchem Satz? Schreibe die Ziffern 1–8 in die richtigen Kästchen.

a ☐ adults   e ☐ disagree
b ☒ _1_ bacon   f ☐ respond
c ☐ bow   g ☐ stare
d ☐ date   h ☐ unfriendly

UNIT 8 Moving images

LESSON 1 The characters seem to speak

1 Höre dir die Tonaufnahme an und ordne die Berufe den richtigen Personen zu. Schreibe a–i in die richtigen Kästchen.

1 Alice   [f]
2 Alex   [ ]
3 Adam   [ ]
4 Cathy   [ ]
5 Ben   [ ]
6 Clare   [ ]
7 Steve   [ ]
8 Sophie   [ ]
9 Fran   [ ]

a computer expert
b designer
c film-maker
d inventor
e journalist
f musician
g pilot
h referee
i tourist guide

2 Was machen die Sprecher? Höre dir die Tonaufnahme an und ordne sie der entsprechenden Tätigkeit zu. Schreibe die Ziffern 1–5 in die richtigen Kästchen.

a [ ] arguing
b [ ] offering to do something
c [ ] planning something
d [ ] refusing to do something
e [ ] saving someone

LESSON 2 If you like a boy …

3 Bringe die Buchstaben der Wörter in Klammern in die richtige Reihenfolge. Schreibe die Wörter in die Lücken. Überprüfe deine Antworten, indem du dir die Tonaufnahme anhörst.

I don't talk about my (1) _____ (slingefe) very much. Sometimes I get (2) _____ (sperdeeds). And sometimes I lose my (3) _____ (rempet) with my family. Yesterday I (4) _____ (thosedu) at my sister. I didn't (5) _____ (name) to, but it just happened. I suppose everyone feels (6) _____ (wond) sometimes.

4 Ergänze die Sätze mit dem richtigen Wort. Überprüfe deine Antworten, indem du dir die Tonaufnahme anhörst.

button ~~chip~~ compare digital information mathematics measure mix square tiny

1 All computers have a _chip_.
2 Can you see this _____ insect on my hand?
3 He isn't good at languages but he's brilliant at science and _____.
4 I don't know the length of this room but we can _____ it.
5 I use a brilliant website to get _____ for my geography projects.
6 If you _____ yellow and blue, you get green.
7 It's a _____ swimming pool. It's three metres wide and three metres long.
8 Put your money in the machine and press the _____.
9 With _____ cameras, you don't need to buy films.
10 You shouldn't _____ him with his brother. They're both nice in different ways.

90

LESSON 4 Describing a process

5 Höre dir die Tonaufnahme an und ordne die Sätze den Bildern zu. Schreibe die Ziffern 1–5 in die richtigen Kästchen.

a ☐

b ☐

c ☐

d ☐

e ☐

6 Lies diese Antworten. Ordne jeden Satz, den du hörst, diesen Antworten zu. Schreibe die Ziffern 1–5 in die richtigen Kästchen.

Antworten

a ☐ I got depressed, you know, really down.

b ☐ I'll have a go.

c ☐ Let me see. Perhaps you should go and see your cousins in Scotland.

d ☐ That's a good question.

e ☐ Yes, I did, but to tell the truth, it wasn't easy.

PRONUNCIATION

Ordne diese Wörter entweder *blow* oder *bossy* zu. Schreibe sie in die richtige Spalte. Überprüfe deine Antworten, indem du dir die Tonaufnahme anhörst.

bone	hotter	offer
contact	knows	process
Covent Garden	model	studio
goes	popular	yellow

/əʊ/ **blow**	/ɒ/ **bossy**
bone	

END OF BOOK QUIZ

Höre dir die Tonaufnahme an. Welches der beiden Wörter passt zu dem jeweiligen Satz? Markiere es mit einem Kringel.

1 wait / ⓦeight
2 won / one
3 meat / meet
4 knew / new
5 you're / your
6 knows / nose
7 there / they're
8 wear / where
9 their / there
10 right / write
11 sea / see
12 here / hear